habiTS of the HEART

habits of the HEART

Practices for Spiritual Seekers

Nancy Steeves

HABITS OF THE HEART
Practices for Spiritual Seekers

Copyright © Nancy Steeves, 2023

All rights reserved. No part of this publication may be reproduced, stored in a retrieval system, or transmitted in any form or by any means, electronic, mechanical, photocopying, recording, or otherwise, without written permission of the author and publisher.

Scripture quotations are from the New Revised Standard Version, © 1989, by the Division of Christian Education of the National Council of the Churches of Christ in the U.S.A. Used by permission. All rights reserved.

Published by Nancy Steeves, Edmonton, Canada
rev.nancy.steeves@gmail.com

Cover art by Amy Loewan, Edmonton, Canada

ISBN:
  Paperback   978-1-77354-463-2
  ebook   978-1-77354-464-9

Publication assistance by

PUBLISHING
PageMaster.ca

For Dawn ~

my beloved partner in life, love,
and every endeavor

and without whom these words
would not have reached a reader's eye

with all my heart and deep gratitude

Contents

Introduction	1
The Practice of Blessing	4
The Practice of Vulnerability	10
The Practice of Collective Compassion	16
The Practice of Resistance	23
The Practice of Listening	28
The Practice of Creating Community	32
The Practice of Speaking Truth	38
The Practice of Creativity	44
The Practice of Resilience	50
The Practice of Communion	54
The Practice of Hope	59
The Practice of Wonder	64
The Practice of Letting Go	69
The Practice of Deepening	75
The Practice of Pausing	79
The Practice of Singing	84
The Practice of Recognition	87
The Practice of Unsettling	94

The Practice of Unshielding 101

The Practice of Kinship 108

The Practice of Curiosity 114

The Practice of Reverence 119

The Practice of Belonging.. 125

The Practice of Turning 132

The Practice of Enchantment.. 137

The Practice of Celebrating Diversity 143

The Practice of Inspiring Compassion 149

The Practice of Engaging Life with Spiritual Depth 154

The Practice of Authenticity.. 159

The Practice of Peacemaking 164

The Practice of Seeking Justice... 169

Epilogue 176

Notes 178

About the Artist... 184

About the Author 185

Introduction

The habits of life form the soul.
~ Honouré de Balzac ~
(1746-1829)

There are so many habits upon which our lives depend. I'm not sure we even think to call them *habits* because they aren't practices we consciously choose. But if our hearts didn't have the habit of beating and resting, and our lungs didn't have the habit of filling with air and emptying carbon dioxide from our bodies, we wouldn't have the habit of living.

Yet not all habits are lifegiving. There are dangerous ones that are so hard to break, like a drug habit or an alcohol addiction. There are the benign habits we try to break like biting our nails. It is a curious thing in our language that we name the distinctive clothing worn by some members of religious orders a "habit." It is an evocative name for a simple garment that covers most of the body, signifying that someone is living specific vows and commitments. Perhaps, in a very real sense, all habits are worn. We are clad in patterns of thoughts, actions, and behaviours that shape how we spend our time and where we place our energy.

In the pages that follow, I am sharing the fruit of a habit that has been a primary part of my vocational life for much of the last 40 years. I have been privileged to have so many opportunities week after week, month after month, year after year to speak into the lives of generously attentive listeners with whom I have shared life in spiritual communities. For most of the last 20 years, I have had the good fortune to be a member of the ministry team of Southminster-Steinhauer United Church (SSUC) in Edmonton and now also in Saskatoon.[1]

I've had a place to speak at the table for more Sundays than I can count – to share my insights, ponderings, questions, hopes, and fears. Over the years, I have cultivated this habit of reflecting on the texts of the natural world, my lived experiences, music, art, literature, poetry, science, film, and the ancient texts of my Judeo-Christian tradition. I've been invited to regularly synthesize and articulate what I find to be true and worthy of our best intentions and energies. The art and craft of writing and speaking Sunday reflections has been a significant spiritual practice for me. I've been both terrified and gratified by the expectation and invitation to speak into and out of the thick of life together.

In my reflections, I have made a habit of capitalizing the word *Earth* to remind myself that our planetary home is a subject with which I am in relationship. For me, *Earth* is not an object which is so often unintentionally suggested by using the definite article in referring to our planet as *the earth*. In a similar way, with the exception of being faithful to quotations, I have made a habit of using the lower case 'g' when referring to any deity I reference in exploring these ancient stories. This practice has helped me to find wisdom that was lost to me in the personification of the god of the Judeo-Christian tradition. It is my intention not to reinforce the theistic understanding that has defined and confined the meaning of these texts.

Introduction

This collection of reflections was offered Sunday by Sunday over the course of 2015 within the gracious circle of my spiritual community of SSUC. These words would have remained in a filing cabinet drawer were it not for the support, encouragement, effort, dedication, and gifts of my beloved spouse, Dawn Waring. In more ways than I can begin to name, this project would have been impossible without her careful eye, editing and research skills, generosity of time, and capacity to attend to the details great and small. It is truly a collaboration. I am deeply indebted to Clair Woodbury for the hours of initiating, organizing, and editing he undertook to help turn words intended for the ears of listeners into ones for the eyes of readers. I offer my heartfelt appreciation to Joyce Madsen, Marion Briggs, and Heather Marshall for their careful and critical reading of this work so that these words might find their best voice. I am also grateful to the community of SSUC and the support of my teammate Christopher New for sabbatical time, even in the midst of a global pandemic. With this gift of time, I have been able to revisit these reflections and bring them to print.

I am honoured by the skill, generosity, and commitment of Amy Loewan in providing her original artwork and cover design for this collection. Her art has been a source of inspiration to me along with the gift of her friendship. Amy is an award-winning multidisciplinary artist and passionate art instructor based in Edmonton, Alberta. Much of her work has been created to promote the values of peace, harmony, and understanding.

It is my hope that in some small way, these reflections on ancient stories and our own lived wisdom will contribute to your quest for what you must make habitual to live soulfully – to inhabit your days in ways that are meaningful and significant.

Vancouver Island, British Columbia
March 2022

The Practice of Blessing

If you can't bless it, get ready to make it new.

~ Marge Piercy ~
"The art of blessing the day"

Jacob was left alone; and a man wrestled with him until daybreak. When the man saw that he did not prevail against Jacob, he struck him on the hip socket; and Jacob's hip was put out of joint as he wrestled with him. Then he said, "Let me go, for the day is breaking." But Jacob said, "I will not let you go, unless you bless me." So he said to him, "What is your name?" And he said, "Jacob." Then the man said, "You shall no longer be called Jacob, but Israel ..." And there he blessed him. Genesis 32:24-29

The turning of time into a new year has traditionally invited us to make resolutions. You know the kind of thing I mean – eat better, lose weight, exercise more, pay down debt, stop smoking, have more balance in life, spend more time with the people we love and things that matter. We could create a long list of resolutions together, new intentions we set for ourselves each year to give up habits we would like to lose or take up others we want to cultivate. Someone once told me that it takes thirty days to make a new habit, but only four days of neglect to lose it.

I must admit that I am not a big fan of New Year's resolutions. Perhaps that just reflects my score card! If I were better at keeping them, maybe I'd be more of a fan. I guess they've never been my thing because they feel like goals which seem to be mostly measured by achievement or failure.

What if each new page on the calendar was an opportunity to do what so many businesses do at the outset of a new year when they take inventory? What if each new day was an opportunity to take stock and intentionally focus on the treasures and pleasures that surround us? Could it be a time to consider what sits on the shelves of our lives that has become invisible to us, a time to investigate the cupboards and closets where we have packed our memories away for so long that we have actually forgotten some of the things we have? Perhaps if we were to take stock, we might discover resources that are in abundance in our lives.

To take such an inventory is not about creating a ledger of assets and liabilities nor about building a balance sheet. It is about giving our attention to what makes our life possible. It is focussing on what makes our life meaningful, rediscovering the great and wonderful and the small and simple things on which our lives are utterly dependent.

When did we last bless the tree that stands in our yard with such strength and beauty, giving us shade from the heat of summer and co-conspiring with us in the great oxygen/carbon dioxide exchange? When did we last bless the sun for the gift of its warmth and its capacity to lift our spirits with its brightness? When did we last bless the soil that opens to feed us or the plants and animals that give their lives to satisfy our hunger? When did we last bless gravity for keeping us upright and grounded? When did we last bless the air in our lungs for giving us another moment of being? When did we last bless the child that made us laugh, the stranger who offered a simple kindness, the loved one who graces our lives with companionship and sacrifice? How is it that we can bless a sneeze with such ease and neglect to bless all the elements, creatures, and tiny graces that touch our lives each day?

Some years ago, someone very important in my life received a letter from her father. He was in the final months of his life and had used his limited energy and time to write a very careful and thoughtful letter to each of his children and to his wife. He spoke of his love for them; he offered his wisdom and advice about their futures. He forgave a loan to one of his daughters. He shared his pride in their accomplishments but even more importantly in the quality of human character he saw in each of them. He blessed a relationship that he had previously refused to accept. He spoke of his deep gratitude for the family with which he had been privileged to share his life. There was no lament that he would not live to see his 69th birthday, that retirement had been abbreviated. There was no complaint that his illness was unfair or that life had been unkind. His letter was an inventory of all that had made life meaningful. He would not have considered himself to be a religious man, but in truth, what he was doing in writing these letters was a deeply spiritual practice. It was the art and act of blessing.

Blessing is an ancient practice in so many spiritual traditions. In the scriptures of the Jewish and Christian traditions, you'd be hard pressed to find a word used more often than "bless." It seems to be one of the Bible's favourite words. Patriarchs bless their eldest sons. Everyone blesses their good fortunes again and again. The rain is blessed for falling, the sun for shining, the earth for producing an abundance of food. The god they understand to be the author of their lives and destinies is blessed. Jesus of Nazareth blesses children, blesses bread, blesses his followers, and blesses those who seem not to have a single blessing to their name. He calls the poor, the grieving, the hungry, the persecuted, and the humble *blessed*.

Many spiritual traditions have crafted rituals to bless homes, pets, children, bicycles, food, relationships, as well as a thousand other things under the sun. We've turned this simple spiritual practice that was originally something anyone and everyone could do into a priestly function to be performed by professionals. But the art and act of blessing is a habit we all need to cultivate for the health of our heart and the health of our world. What we bless, we won't mindlessly consume. Those whom we bless, we won't neglect or use. When we bless, we will not miss the holiness that is within the most ordinary moments and relationships of our lives. And wherever we bless, we will find the sacredness in life.

There will always be some things in life that are difficult to bless. Like the archetypal character Jacob, we will be hurt by life, by strangers and loved ones, by faces we recognize and ones we don't. We will be hurt by our struggles and wounded by our experiences. We will be challenged, as the characters in the ancient story were challenged, to bless those we have wounded and to be blessed by our wounds and our assailants.

The story the Genesis narrative gives us suggests they gave their blessing in a way that makes it sound almost automatic and effortless. In the succinct way of stories, it seems as simple as Jacob asking for the stranger's blessing, having a conversation about each other's name, and that was it. The blessing appears to be offered and received as though neither of them had to give it a second thought. Stories can compress the realities of life into such an economy of words that we are deceived by a simplicity that isn't there.

I wonder if some of the wisdom in this story might be that our hurts and wounds *do* seek our blessing. The unwelcome and unbidden things in our lives *do* challenge us to find the sacredness in them or imbue them with a holiness that will determine how we walk with them. I hear in this story, as I hear in life, the possibility of blessing or cursing the inevitable intrusions of hurt and change in our lives.

Maybe it took Jacob a lot of hindsight not only to receive the blessing of this stranger but to give this one who had wounded him his blessing. Maybe it took time and insight for Jacob to release his hold on the hurt and give his blessing to something that altered his future. Or maybe he had lived long enough to know what happens when we withhold our blessing and live inside the curse of regret and the world of what-ifs.

The story fails to tell us that the practice of blessing is habit forming. It takes a lifetime to train the heart to bless both the joy and pain, the gifts and challenges of life, the obvious and the hidden inventory on which our life depends. We don't need to wait until the closing chapters of life to bless one another. We don't need to wait until we are in danger of losing a beloved tree or treasure to bless it. We don't need a new year to start a new habit. We just need a new breath to start a new habit. It doesn't take any special words or incantations to begin the spiritual practice of blessing. All we need to do is attend to what gives our life beauty and meaning, and then bless it, thank it, and praise it just for being what it is. Chances are we will find ourselves to be more alive. So, let's find something our eyes see, our ears hear, our hands touch, or our hearts know, and let's practice the art of blessing. It could be habit forming!

This reflection was offered on January 11, 2015.

The Practice of Vulnerability

*When we were children, we used to think that when we
were grown-up, we would no longer be vulnerable.
But to grow up is to accept vulnerability ...
To be alive is to be vulnerable.*

~ Madeleine L'Engle ~
Walking on Water

"Let my life be given me – that is my petition – and the lives of my people – that is my request. For we have been sold, I and my people, to be destroyed, to be killed, and to be annihilated ..." Esther 7:3-4

Do you ever wish life came with signage, like the signs we see on our highways? Before we come to a crossroad in life, wouldn't it be helpful to see a sign warning us of an "important intersection ahead?" It might give us time to prepare for decisions we're going to have to make. Or if we saw the sign "slow down," like we see in school and playground zones, we might pay attention to things we are certain to miss in life because we don't gear down or use our brakes. If we were cautioned about "sharp curves ahead," we might be more careful while navigating the next piece of life's road. We might be a bit more patient with each other if we saw a "no passing" sign or one that said, "yield to oncoming traffic."

The thing is, if these were signs posted on the road through life, they'd all be obscured by the one that reads, "vulnerability ahead." This is the truth of life. It's always there. It is the nature of being alive. If we are breathing, we are vulnerable – to hope and despair, to joy and pain, to gain and loss, to love and fear, to acceptance and rejection, to health and disease, to be being understood and being misunderstood.

Since 9/11, the western world has become obsessed with security. We have been seduced into thinking that with increased surveillance, more weapons, expanded powers to detain, or enhanced equipment to search our bodies, our luggage, our homes and offices, we will be safer. Most of the developing world knows that security is an illusion. To live is to be at risk. Life challenges us to learn to live with our vulnerability.

It is ironic that it takes practice to be vulnerable. It is like saying that it takes practice to breathe. In one sense, that is a ridiculous assertion. We just breathe. We are just vulnerable.

But there are countless masters who will teach us how to really breathe, to consciously breathe. Isn't this much of the appeal of yoga and so many forms of meditation?

There are also countless teachers of vulnerability, those who invite us to stop hiding from ourselves and each other and to face our fears. They call forth the hidden in us and welcome the real me and the real you. There are those who open their own experience to us with such honesty and rawness that we find it impossible not to meet their vulnerability with our own.

In the literature of the ancient world, Esther is one of those teachers for me. The story that bears her name isn't history, although it tells a story that has been repeated many times in history. It is a legend that was written to be re-enacted during the Jewish festival of Purim, the annual feast in the Jewish tradition that celebrates the survival of a people and their faith against all odds. It is a fable in which the tables are turned, where the ones without power win and the powerful are punished by the very means they intended to inflict on others. It is a story that celebrates a crafty victory over blatant patriarchy, abusive political power, religious intolerance, and overt racism.

In the world of the story, Esther is an orphan raised by her uncle. She comes to be queen in Persia by winning a beauty contest after the previous queen lost that throne and her life by refusing to dance for the king and his drunken guests at a party that was already seven days old. Esther comes to the throne with a secret. She is a member of an ethnic and religious minority that becomes the target of a racist bureaucrat and a complicit king. The book of Esther is one of only two in the Bible to bear the name of a woman, and it is one of only two books that doesn't use the word "God" at all.

Like many stories, not all its lessons are ones to emulate. It is a story that perpetuates gender stereotypes and a deep-rooted patriarchy. It is a story of scheming and manipulating, racism and revenge. It is a tale where victory is celebrated with violence.

It is also a story that turns on the vulnerability of its heroine. Esther could have remained silent and saved herself, while other Jews were hung on Haman's gallows. She could have kept her secret safe and her identity hidden by refusing to "come out" as Jewish. She could have used some scheme, rather than risking the truth, as a way of manipulating the king into reversing the law that put her people in peril. The story celebrates her courage, but it is really her vulnerability that determines the plot. She puts herself at risk by exposing herself as one of those targeted by Haman's racial profiling and program of genocide, a program approved by the king, her husband. Unwittingly, her husband had signed her death warrant.

That's the power of hundreds of stories that have been shared in *The Trevor Project,* stories told to empower LGBTQ2S+ young people with the knowledge that life gets better.[2] Celebrities, presidents, police officers, musicians, employees of Facebook and Apple and hundreds of other companies have participated. These are people who have given up their privacy, have felt again the pain and shame brought down on them by parents and peers, have been vulnerable to their own emotions, and have put their experience online for the world to see.

These courageous, vulnerable individuals have shared their own experiences of being bullied, put down, rejected, or even suicidal. They have exposed themselves and their own vulnerability in the hopes of saving others who may not see any light in their darkness.

Whatever our gender, our sexual orientation, our gender identity, our race, or our religion, we are as easily misled as Elsa's character in the movie *Frozen*.[3] We are led to conceal ourselves and neglect the power to be who we are – to hide the best or worst of ourselves for fear that we will not be accepted. We are led to wall ourselves off in a sense of shame or blame. Like Elsa, we try to keep ourselves from feeling our fear and are misled into believing that the strong don't cry. We are Elsa in search of the Esther within us.

Somehow, what was as natural as breathing in our infancy takes practice as we mature. Vulnerability is a habit the heart must relearn if we are to be truly alive. That is the hard lesson Elsa's character had to learn in the world of the film. That is the noble lesson Esther's character teaches in the ancient story. Vulnerability is the oxygen of the spirit. As spiritual beings in a human experience,[4] we are in danger of depriving our spirits of the oxygen we need in our efforts to remain safe and secure. Ironically, our best hope for security comes out of our courage to be vulnerable to each other. In our vulnerability, we may find our shared humanity. I like to think that Esther's vulnerability inspired the king to be vulnerable as well, to admit his mistake and reverse his death edict. By risking appearing to be weak, the king exercised a strength of leadership not previously seen in the story.

One of the reasons we gather as a spiritual community is to develop the habits of the heart that will empower us to be our highest and best selves. We come into the safety of our spiritual communities to learn to be vulnerable to our tears and fears, to our hopes and dreams, to the gift of our diversity, to the wisdom that challenges the conventions so many in our society have accepted. Like Elsa, who accepted the fear-filled counsel of her father, we are easily encouraged to hide our true self, even from the ones who love us most.

The spiritual community of SSUC has offered a safe place to be one's true self. Over the years that the SSUC congregation has been committed to being an affirming spiritual community, we have witnessed the courage of many who have risked being vulnerable, daring to share their experiences of hurt and rejection. They have risked being vulnerable to losing relationships with loved ones to be in right relationship with themselves. They have risked taking their place in a faith community after having known the judgment and exclusion of family, friends, and other faith communities.

May we find the courage of Esther and the participants in *The Trevor Project* to risk opening our hearts and lives to one another. The courage of one to be vulnerable is an invitation to another to risk being more fully known and more deeply cherished. Vulnerability is a sacred trust which has the power to create the world we dream of where we are *all* free to be because *each* is free to be. It is a spiritual practice upon which authentic community depends.

> *This reflection was offered on January 25, 2015, on the 16th anniversary of the congregation's commitment to be a community of welcome, acceptance, and safety for gay, lesbian, bisexual, transgender, non-binary, two-spirit, queer, questioning, and heterosexual persons.*

The Practice of Collective Compassion

The principle of compassion lies at the heart of all religious, ethical and spiritual traditions, calling us always to treat all others as we wish to be treated ourselves. Compassion impels us to work tirelessly to alleviate the suffering of our fellow creatures, to dethrone ourselves from the centre of our world and put another there, and to honour the inviolable sanctity of every single human being, treating everybody, without exception, with absolute justice, equity and respect.[5]

~ Charter for Compassion ~

[Jesus] said to them, "Come away to a deserted place all by yourselves and rest a while." For many were coming and going, and they had no leisure even to eat. And they went away in the boat to a deserted place by themselves. Now many saw them going and recognized them, and they hurried there on foot from all the towns and arrived ahead of them. As he went ashore, he saw a great crowd; and he had compassion for them, because they were like sheep without a shepherd; and he began to teach them many things. When it grew late, his disciples came to him and *said, "This is a deserted place, and the hour is now very late; send them away so that they may go into the surrounding country and villages and buy something for themselves to eat." But he answered them, "You give them something to eat." They said to him, "Are we to go and buy two hundred denarii worth of bread, and give it to them to eat?" And he said to them, "How many loaves have you? Go and see." When they had found out, they said, "Five, and two fish." Then he ordered them to get all the people to sit down in groups on the green grass. So they sat down in groups of hundreds and of fifties. Taking the five loaves and the two fish, he looked up to heaven, and blessed and broke the loaves, and gave them to his disciples to set before the people; and he divided the two fish among them all. And all ate and were filled; and they took up twelve baskets full of broken pieces and of the fish.* Mark 6:31-43

It's been over half a century since 8,000 men, women, and children left Selma, Alabama, to march 54 miles over five days to arrive on the steps of the state capital in Montgomery, Alabama. On the final day of that march, their numbers had grown to more than 25,000 people: young and old, black and white, men and women, all stood together as a community. They were tired and hungry: tired of being poor and hungry for justice; tired of the right to vote being denied on the basis of colour, and hungry for all to have a voice in electing their leaders; tired of being freed from the evils of slavery only to be enslaved in segregation, and hungry for equality and dignity. It had been 10 years earlier in Montgomery, Alabama, that a brave Black woman had been too tired to walk to the back of the bus. Rosa Parks took her seat near the front of the bus. She was tired of being a second-class citizen and hungry for freedom, the freedom just to be.

Though segregation was officially outlawed by 1965, one of the great barriers to equality was the inability of African Americans to succeed in registering to vote, especially in states like Alabama. The march to demand that right began three times. The first time there were just a few hundred African Americans, tired of being denied the freedoms of their democracy and hungry for inclusion. They were met by utter cruelty on the George Pettus Bridge where local and state police beat and brutalized them, forcing them back to Selma.

Many white people from across the United States, and some from Canada, were moved with compassion as they watched this horror broadcast on their TV sets. They responded to the call of Martin Luther King Jr. to come to Selma and march in solidarity with these brave Black Americans. Compassion moved many to place their bodies in danger and their lives at risk to walk alongside their vulnerable Black brothers and sisters in the struggle for equality.

The second attempt to march saw the crowd go to their knees in prayer when they got to the place on the bridge where, on the previous Sunday, Bloody Sunday as it came to be known, they had been violently turned back. To the disappointment of many, King, who was leading the march, determined that it was unsafe to continue and turned the crowd back. Tired of violence and hungry for peace, the organizers eventually succeeded in getting a court order and federal protection for the third attempt that did take them to the steps of the state capital on March 25, 1965. It took a court being moved to compassion and the oval office being moved to action before this march succeeded in enacting a peaceful demonstration, demanding an end to being barred from the voting booth. The march from Selma to Montgomery ultimately resulted in President Johnson signing the Voter's Rights Act five months later.

We still live in a world that is tired and hungry:

- Tired of terror and hungry for respect.
- Tired of poverty and hungry for equity.
- Tired of addictions and hungry for serenity.
- Tired of war and hungry for peace.
- Tired of fouling our nest and hungry for a healthier planet.
- Tired of intolerance and hungry for harmony.
- Tired of violence and hungry for understanding.
- Tired of scandals and hungry for integrity.
- Tired of disease and hungry for all to live to a ripe old age.
- Tired of wait lists and hungry for truly universal access to health care.
- Tired of competition and hungry for co-operation.
- Tired of cruelty and hungry for compassion.

Jesus and his friends knew what it was to live in a world that was tired and hungry. They were tired of being occupied by the Roman Empire and hungry for liberation and independence. They were tired of ten percent of the population controlling ninety percent of the land. They were tired of losing their lands to the burden of debt caused by unfair taxation. They were hungry for a more equitable social arrangement. They were tired of being poor and landless, and hungry for dignity and equality.

Maybe that's why each gospel writer of the first century gives us this story of a community that is tired and hungry. Mark's gospel, the earliest of these writings, even gives us two of these stories, just two chapters apart, with few differences. One is a tired and hungry crowd of 5,000 and the other a crowd of 4,000 men. And what about the women and children? Surely they must have been tired of never being counted and hungry to be seen and heard!

In Mark's story of the 5,000, Jesus and his friends were tired and hungry too. Their attempt to rest and get away from it all failed. By the time they crossed the lake, many others had made their way to the other side on foot. When Jesus saw the crowd, he was moved with compassion, because they were tired of tyranny and hungry for hope, hungry for leadership, hungry for someone or something to trust. They were "like sheep without a shepherd." Instead of taking the day off as he and his friends had planned, he spent the day nourishing spirits with his vision of a new way of living in communion with creation and in community with each other. The day slipped by, night fell, and now they were all bone-tired and desperately hungry.

The friends of Jesus offered their solution: send the crowd away so each could buy their own food. In other words, let them look after themselves. It is a dog-eat-dog world out there, each man, woman, and child for themselves, survival of the fittest. Isn't that the rule of life? Individualism, capitalism, and consumption. Isn't that what makes the world go round? Their solution to the problem of hunger is to send the crowd away to compete as consumers for a scarce commodity, the great economic cure-all of spending our way into feeling better. But some couldn't even spend their way into survival. Compassion requires more than passing off the problem of hunger to the crowd. According to the story, Jesus turned to his friends and said, "You give them something to eat." For Jesus, the need to eat is not a problem to be solved but an opportunity for a crowd to become a community of compassion.

The disciples still don't get it. They ask, "Are we to go and buy bread that will cost us six months' wages and give it to them to eat?" Now they think they have a new problem. Not only do they not have food, but they also don't have money. Where in the middle of nowhere are they supposed to buy bread with money they don't have?

Jesus tried again. "Go find out how much bread you have." Find the resources you have. Investigate the state of the gathered community. Are there some who don't have anything, some who have more than they need, some who have just enough for themselves? When the disciples checked, they found that someone among them they had five loaves and two fish.

Then the story turns on a seemingly innocuous detail. The crowd was reorganized into groups of 50 or 100. Something about that simple act of reconstituting a faceless crowd of thousands into smaller face-to-face communities created conditions of intimacy that bred compassion. The smaller communities sit down with each other on green grass where they can touch the earth that gives and sustains life. Then the story has Jesus celebrate what he has been given. He looks up, blesses and breaks the bread, and gives those five loaves and two fish back to his friends, modelling a possibility for each community to enact. Now what if they each take what they have, celebrate it with gratitude, and share it with each other?

Miracles aren't magic. This memory of the early Christian community is not that Jesus was the maker of wonder bread. It is a memory of the power of community, moved by compassion, to do what it can.

A wise Quaker woman speaking to thousands at an El Salvador rally many years ago in Boston said there are two solutions to powerlessness: do something and do it together.

Isn't that the story of every movement, whether it is the Jesus movement, or the civil rights movement, or any liberation movement? When we are moved by compassion to do something and do it together, then possibilities emerge, powers shift, hearts open, and things change – which is to say, miracles happen.

This is not a story about loaves of bread or fish multiplied before first century eyes. This is a story about what compassion looks like, how it acts. Compassion chooses to hold things for the common good rather than looking out for oneself. Compassion doesn't discriminate between those who have something and those who need something. Jesus and his disciples shared what they had, and that same compassion moved each to share what they had, transforming the crowd into a community. The miracle is that in sharing what they had, there was enough, actually more than enough.

These words travel to us across time and tradition, reminding us that compassion is a habit of the heart. Like every habit, it requires practice. It takes practice to transcend self-interest, to trust we can do something if we act, and we act together, in a tired and hungry world. It takes practice to reframe our conversations from budget deficits to compassion surpluses. It takes practice to see through the law-and-order policies that try to trick us into believing that we will be safer as a society if we just take care of ourselves.

The Selmas everywhere call for our compassion, not just our prayers, not just our money. They ask for our hearts. They ask us to do something and to do it together. This is a time to consider what compassion requires of us. There are people who are tired and hungry, tired of waiting for it to be on earth as it is in heaven, hungry for a community that practices the habit of compassion.

This reflection was offered on February 1, 2015, honouring Black History Month.

The Practice of Resistance

*Do your little bit of good where you are.
It's those little bits of good put together
that overwhelm the world.*

~ Viola Desmond ~

The king of Egypt said to the Hebrew midwives, one of whom was named Shiphrah and the other Puah, "When you act as midwives to the Hebrew women, and see them on the birthstool, if it is a boy, kill him; but if it is a girl, she shall live." But the midwives ... did not do as the king of Egypt commanded them, but they let the boys live. Exodus 1:15-17

Nine years before Rosa Parks resisted taking her seat at the back of the bus in Montgomery, Alabama, and in her weariness took a seat in the white's only section, Viola Desmond was resisting segregation as a Black Canadian. She was born over 100 years ago, one of 15 children her parents raised. As a young woman, she wanted to be a beautician and had to travel to Montreal, Atlantic City, and New York for her training because the local Halifax school refused to admit her as a Canadian of

African descent. After completing her program, she returned to Halifax and established her own business as a beautician, set up a beauty school, and developed her own line of products, which she marketed throughout Nova Scotia.

In 1946, at the age of 32, Viola was in New Glasgow on a business trip when her car broke down, and she had to wait a day for it to be repaired. She chose to pass the time by seeing a movie. She purchased a ticket, asking for a seat on the main floor. After she was seated, the manager of the theatre told her she didn't have the ticket for that seat. She went back to the ticket booth and was advised that they couldn't sell a ticket for a main floor seat to a Black person.

When she returned to her seat and refused to sit in the balcony reserved for "Blacks only," she was forcibly removed, injured, arrested, and jailed overnight. She refused to pay the unjust fine and took the matter to trial. The offense she was charged with was tax evasion because there was a one cent difference in the ticket price between a balcony and main floor seat. That penny of difference was a retail tax. She was convicted without any mention of her race or of the racist policy that created the offense. Her story received very little notice outside of Nova Scotia at the time but eventually became one of the milestone acts of resistance that led to the elimination of segregation in that province. In 2010, she was granted a pardon, 45 years after her death.

In 2003, another young woman, Rachel Corrie, was a student in her senior year at The Evergreen State College when she went to Gaza as a volunteer with International Solidarity Movement (ISM). She was killed by a bulldozer operated by an Israeli soldier on a mission to demolish a Palestinian home in Gaza. During a peaceful act of resistance, as she and others stood wearing brightly coloured vests and communicating with bullhorns, she was crushed to death in the act of protesting the unjust policies that make Palestinian families homeless.[6]

These two women are among the contemporary midwives who refuse to deal in death: the death of dignity, equality, and shelter. They refuse to acquiesce, be complicit, or remain silent in the face of injustice. They are the "Shiphrah" and "Puah" of the twentieth and twenty-first centuries, refusing to comply with laws, policies, and regulations which are blatantly senseless or unjust. They act, accepting the risk of adverse consequences, because a higher moral authority has laid claim to their hearts.

The ancient Exodus story inspired the anti-slavery movement, the anti-segregation movement, the civil rights movement, and so many activist movements for social change. You hear echoes of this foundational story of the Jewish tradition in the songs that carried these liberation movements. Most of the African American spirituals draw images from this ancient archetypal story of freedom. This story isn't history. It is the classic tale of oppression and freedom which the human community continues to experience again and again.

The book of Exodus opens with a story of grassroots resistance to a policy that begins in oppression and ends in genocide. It is the story of a fearful lawmaker who is threatened by the potential that those he identifies as the *other* may become the majority and have the capacity to remove him from power. The Pharaoh of the day fears that the exploited labour force of migrants may reach a point where they no longer simply accept their lot in life. In the celebrated Exodus narrative, we hear the perennial story of those who will find ways to resist, subvert, confront, and challenge the status quo of injustice and inhumanity.

In the world of this ancient story, it all begins with two women who refuse to carry out the king's orders to kill the male children of the underclass. They find a disguise for their direct defiance with a smoke screen excuse that they just weren't there in time to prevent these children from being born alive. We learn little about the identity of these midwives. Are they Egyptian midwives to Hebrew women or are they Hebrew women who serve as midwives to their own? We also never learn their fate. What lives on in the story is their model of a peaceful, creative civil disobedience that was highly effective in subverting the Pharaoh's inhumane order.

A character named Moses ultimately gets all the credit for leading the liberation, but really the movement is birthed by the acts of resistance of these midwives, along with three other women. The first resistor is a mother who placed her child in a basket in the river to be watched by his sister until another woman (the daughter of the one who ordered this child and all others like him to be killed) drew him out of the water and raised him as her own child. Each was an activist in her own right. Each did what she could to resist and subvert the unjust law.

These women are among the true radicals – those who have worked for progressive change in our world, not those who are indoctrinated by hatred and schooled in violence or whose minds, bodies, or spirits are broken by poverty, war, occupation, oppression, or imprisonment.

Surely Jesus of Nazareth was a radical. He challenged the authority of his own religious leaders, raging against their exploitation of the poor and their complicity with the occupying force in making peasants landless. He challenged the accepted wisdom that peace is won by war, promoting a peace that arises out of justice. And Jesus was killed for his subversive resistance.

He wasn't executed because he was an inspiring teacher, a compassionate healer, or a good preacher. Jesus was accused of treason and executed in a public humiliation to deter resistance to the unjust rule of an empire in bed with a religious institution of the first century. Undoubtedly, media today would bill it as the execution of a terrorist, a radical.

He was a midwife to a vision of mutuality, equality, and justice in the good company of Shiphrah and Puah, and so many others before him and after him, who were willing to risk whatever it takes to resist injustice and challenge the evils of cruelty and inhumanity. As heirs of the Judeo-Christian tradition, this is our inheritance.

Resistance is a spiritual practice. We have many mentors who have taught us to seek justice and resist evil and the distortions of our humanity. In the company of so many who have endured so much injustice, change has come. And change will come as it always has, midwifed by those who have the courage to stand against what is unfair, unkind, and unjust, even when it is lawful.

Our indigenous brothers and sisters are teaching us a way to confront inequity in *Idle No More*. Our youth are showing their resistance in the *Occupy* movement. Environmental and animal rights activists are demonstrating around the world. There are many ways to resist: by what we buy and what we refuse to buy, by how we place our vote as citizens and shareholders, by how we invest or divest our money, by how we refuse to be silent and how and where we place our voice and our very lives. We have countless opportunities to cultivate the practice of resistance. And it can make a world of difference.

This reflection was offered on February 8, 2015.

The Practice of Listening

The first duty of love is to listen.

~ Paul Tillich ~
Love, Power, and Justice

At Gibeon the Lord appeared to Solomon in a dream by night; and God said, "Ask what I should give you." And Solomon said, "... Give your servant a hearing heart[7] to govern your people, to discern between good and evil ..."
1 Kings 3:5-6, 9

In the world of the ancient story, Solomon wasn't born to be king. It really wasn't in the cards for him. He couldn't have anticipated being the one to occupy the throne of ancient Israel since he wasn't favoured by his father, the ruling king, as the leading candidate for the job. Similarly, he wasn't the first choice of General Joab, the head of the military, whose support he would need if he was going to manage to keep the job. He wasn't the king's oldest son, but he was his mother's favourite. And his mother, Bathsheba, was his father's favourite wife. So, it was his mother who succeeded in persuading her husband, and Solomon was reluctantly given the job.

Then reality set in. We see him slipping into his soft cotton sheets, thanks to the dowry of his Egyptian wife, a marriage of convenience and alliance. But despite the comforts of kingship, he hasn't slept since the coronation. He's as terrified as the stuttering King George VI but for a very different reason. He is sitting on Israel's throne in the shadow of his famous father, King David. He is the very unfortunate successor of the one who will always be remembered as Israel's favourite king.

Both he and his nation are still grieving, as he climbs onto the throne. No one wants Solomon to be king – they want another "David" to be their king. It doesn't take Solomon very long to figure out that it is going to take more than a fancy crown and a cushy throne to keep house and home together, to ward off Israel's invaders and make strategic friends among his Middle Eastern neighbours. Some 3,000 years ago, during Solomon's reign, Israel was a bridge of land between Asia, Africa, and Europe. It was a challenging part of the world where conflict and conquest were always both the fabric of history and on the horizon.

He has plenty of reasons to be sleepless in Jerusalem. After way too many restless nights in the palace, he opts for fresh air and perspective at Israel's Meech Lake, their Camp David. He heads for the royal getaway at Gibeon. We meet him, in the world of the story, just as he has found deep and dream-filled sleep at his country retreat, the first good night's sleep he has had in who knows how long.

In the world of his dreams, he is a young boy approaching a magnificent throne. The one who sits on the throne appears to be a wizard or genie who is prepared to grant him, not three, but just one wish. And he can ask for anything under the sun. In this dream, someone is addressing *him*. Someone is interested in him and wants to know something about him. Someone recognizes that he is searching for something that will give him the confidence to take his place and lead well.

For weeks now, he has been listening to the chatter of his anxieties and the noise of his fears. His insecurities have probably been screaming at him for his whole life. Feeling small and insignificant, in this dream he sees himself as a child invited to speak his most intimate truth, to share the desire of his heart. I wonder if anyone had ever offered him an opportunity like this before. I wonder if this is the first time he has been invited to be heard. We hardly need Freud or Jung to tell us what's going on with this guy. His dream reveals much about his relationship with each of his parents and the insecurities he holds as he assumes responsibility for leadership.

Feeling entirely unequal to the task of governing this great nation, Solomon's single wish is spoken as his deepest prayer: "Give your servant a hearing heart to govern your people, to discern between good and evil." How I wish this was the prayer that opened each sitting of our Parliament, our legislative assembly, city council, and our courts.

A hearing heart! Who would have thought that the silk-clad Solomon, the insecure and uncertain national leader, the first of the big-time spenders with a court that consumed a daily menu that could feed an entire city – who would have thought that the deepest desire of Solomon's heart would be for a new heart, a heart that could hear? Now you know what to get for the person who has everything. Or is it for the person who appears to have everything, or the one who has everything except a solid sense of themselves?

Perhaps deep in Solomon's unconscious he knew that fear has a way of dulling our senses. Insecurity has a way of misdirecting our thoughts. Given the chance to ask for anything, he seeks an increase in his capacity to hear, to hear not just with his ears but that he might hear with his heart.

The evolutionary genius of survival may require an anatomical adjustment. The survival of the human species may well depend on shortening the distance between our ears and our hearts. Our ears may be adequate to the task of hearing but listening requires hearts that can hear.

Imagine what could happen if our hearts could hear what our ears hear. We'd have more liberation and less oppression, more justice and less charity, more sharing and less hunger, more giving and less accumulating. We'd have more respect for diversity and less tolerance for discrimination. We'd have more peace and less war. We'd have more conversation and less contempt. If our hearts could hear what our ears hear, we'd have more understanding and less prejudice, more empathy and fewer opinions. We'd have more questions and fewer answers. We'd have more mutuality and less domination, more love and less fear. We'd know less, but we'd feel more. We'd cry more, and we'd laugh longer. Imagine a spiritual community of hearing hearts!

To listen is to risk being changed forever. To truly listen is a spiritual practice. If we take each encounter as an opportunity for our hearts to hear, chances are we will never be the same again.

This reflection was offered on March 8, 2015.

The Practice of Creating Community

If you want to go fast, go alone.
If you want to go far, go together.

~ African Proverb ~

All who believed were together and had all things in common; they would sell their possessions and goods and distribute the proceeds to all, as any had need. Day by day, as they spent much time together in the temple, they broke bread at home and ate their food with glad and generous hearts. Acts 2:44-46

In the world of the film, *Unfinished Song,* Arthur is a grumpy old man married to a woman everybody loves.[8] For reasons we never quite know, he is estranged from his son and adores his granddaughter. Anger is the only emotion he seems to know how to express. We watch him in the deep loneliness of anticipating and then experiencing the grief of losing his wife – the love of his life and the only person who seems to truly understand him.

In the months leading up to her death, Marion finds great joy and meaningful community singing in a seniors' choir. The friendship, care, and support that she experiences in this choir companions her in her dying and helps her give expression to what matters most to her as she faces her death.

But the story is really Arthur's story. It is a tale of the transforming power of community. After Marion's death, Arthur joins the unconventional choir. Through making music with others, Arthur is altered from being an angry loner to a contributing member of a caring community. Even his face softens as his heart opens to his own pain and to the joy and pain of others. The persistence and care of Elizabeth, the young choir director, and an accepting and generous group of choristers help him find his voice and take his place in the community they create together.

Arthur's story is one of *radicalization*. Unfortunately, that word has come to be associated most often with disturbed, deluded, deceived, disillusioned, or disadvantaged young men and women who have been recruited to anger and hatred by global inequities, dangerous religious literalism, or political extremism. We have allowed this important word to be hijacked, taken hostage, and used for another purpose.

What could be more *radical* than a group of devout first century Jews living in Roman occupied Palestine, choosing to sell their personal possessions and hold all things in common to be shared and distributed on the basis of need? What could be more *radical* than the resurrection of these defeated disciples of an unauthorized and itinerant rabbi named Jesus who had been executed by the empire with the help of the religious authorities? These followers had risen out of the ashes of their disappointment to re-organize themselves economically, spiritually, and socially. They gathered daily in synagogues that didn't know what to make of them. In sharing meals with each other, they found wonder and generosity in the community they were creating together.

They would be highly suspect in the twenty-first century and branded as socialists or communists. They might even be targeted as potential terrorists because what they were about was so counter to our culture. At best, they would be deemed unpatriotic. In their rejection of capitalism, they would be viewed as enemies of the state.

What could be more *radical* for these followers of Jesus than to organize themselves as a counter economy in opposition to the dominant economy of the Roman empire? The imperial way has always fostered the concentration of wealth in the hands of the few at the expense and exploitation of the many. The people of this new way are pooling resources and re-distributing them according to need. They are taking care of one another, and the quality of the community they create attracts more and more members. Inspired by the teachings of their leader who had cultivated a counterculture – a beloved community Jesus called "the kingdom of God" – they continued to build a movement that opposed the values of imperial power.

These are our spiritual ancestors, the pioneers of a way of life that was rooted in many of the values and traditions of ancient Judaism and radicalized by the teaching and spiritual practices of Jesus of Nazareth. We are the spiritual heirs of those who were radicalized by his vision of love, justice, equity, mutuality, freedom, and peace. To be a radical is to arise from or return to the root of something, to undergo an extreme change from accepted or traditional norms. If we know anything about the teachings of Jesus, we know that he challenged conventional wisdom and subverted generally accepted norms with his parables.

Again and again we hear this pattern in the teachings attributed to Jesus: *You have heard it said* murder will be judged, *but I say to you,* so will anger. *You have heard it said* unfaithfulness destroys relationship, *but I say to you*, address your thoughts, and your actions will take care of themselves. *You have heard it said* love your neighbour and hate your enemy, *but I say to you,* love your enemies and pray for those who harm you.⁹ If that isn't radical, if that isn't an extreme change from widely held inherited understandings, I don't know what is. These revisions to the received tradition called for higher ethical standards of compassion, generosity, and justice.

The empire succeeded in killing the teacher but not the teaching. It isn't surprising that those who were inspired by the community that formed around Jesus organized in unimagined new ways after his death: selling their possessions, holding all things in common, distributing according to need, gathering as spiritual community in the synagogues and in homes to share food and hope with each other. As these practices characterized their life together, their glad and generous hearts drew others to join them every day. Now that's radical!

We are their descendants; there is much we hold in common that we acknowledge in the baptismal commitments we make when we celebrate new life and extend an invitation to participate in our collective quest. We are spiritual seekers united in community with a consciousness of an all-encompassing spirit in which we live and move and have our being. We are inspired by the teachings of Jesus of Nazareth and find wisdom in the natural world, in literature, science, and the arts, and in all the great teachers, both ancient and contemporary. We are those who seek to live with hearts open to the spirit of life within us and among us – open to the wounds and joys of creation and to the needs of the world. We are those who seek to celebrate the sacredness of life, to live with respect in creation, to love and serve others, to seek justice and resist the distortions of goodness.[10] We hold in common our intentions to celebrate diversity, make a difference, inspire compassion, engage life with spiritual depth, and explore our spiritual life beyond the conventional paths that orthodoxy has laid.[11]

Do we not hold in common a commitment to Earth, our home and to the values expressed in the *Earth Charter*: respect for nature, universal human rights, economic justice, and a culture of peace?[12] Do we not hold in common a commitment to affirm the dignity and inherent worth of each person, whatever their gender, race, sexual orientation, gender identity, education, economic situation, language, culture, or religion?[13] Do we not hold in common a commitment to share the joys of life and the burdens of living and dying by expressing our care in a myriad of ways? Do we not hold in common a commitment to use our multi-purpose facility hospitably by hosting programs offered by other organizations and agencies, employing our collective resources toward all that serves social justice and equity for all?[14]

Immersed in a culture of individualism and consumption, we congregate to nurture common values in much the same spirit as our radical spiritual ancestors. If we are to be faithful to the legacy we have received, we are compelled to cultivate the spiritual practices which train our hearts to think beyond the singular, to teach our hearts to create a commonwealth of compassion instead of a competitive culture of individualism.

Again and again, I witness how we hold one another in our times of grief and our times of gladness, in our abundance and in our need, in our strength and in our vulnerability, in the hopes and fears that we face. It takes practice to teach our hearts the habits that create the kind of community that will hold us in the buoyancy of who we are together, as Marion was held in *Unfinished Song*. Can we allow ourselves to be transformed by a caring and committed community as Arthur was in the world of the film? It takes practice to be radicalized as followers of Jesus of Nazareth – to become an affirming and inclusive spiritual community of seekers united in a quest for more light and greater love.

This reflection was offered on March 15, 2015.

The Practice of Speaking Truth

*In a time of universal deceit,
telling the truth is a revolutionary act.*

~ Attributed to George Orwell ~

A large crowd followed [Jesus] and pressed in on him. Now there was a woman who had been suffering from hemorrhages for twelve years. She had endured much under many physicians, and had spent all that she had; and she was no better, but rather grew worse. She had heard about Jesus, and came up behind him in the crowd and touched his cloak, for she said, "If I but touch his clothes, I will be made well." Immediately her hemorrhage stopped; and she felt in her body that she was healed of her disease. Immediately aware that power had gone forth from him, Jesus turned about in the crowd and said, "Who touched my clothes?" ... The woman, knowing what had happened to her, came in fear and trembling, fell down before him, and told him the whole truth. He said to her, "Daughter, your faith has made you well ..." Mark 5:24-30, 33-34

Speaking Truth

Several years ago, I came across four rules for living. They were pithy statements that really resonated as wisdom for me. They seemed simple enough on the surface. I transcribed these directives into my daytimer to keep them on my eyeball. Every year when I start a new calendar, I rewrite these phrases to remind me to keep trying to practice these four intentions for living. This version is attributed to a US educator and writer, Angeles Arrien: show up, pay attention, tell the truth, and don't be attached to the results.[15]

I have found myself thinking about these rules a lot recently, recognizing that they are like a ladder I am invited to climb. These habits are listed in ascending order of difficulty, each one is a little harder than the one that came before. I find it easier to show up than to pay attention. I find it even harder to tell the truth when my truth may not be what someone wants to hear or when it seems to stand in opposition to theirs. Breaking my attachment to results is the most challenging of all.

This week invited me into several conversations in which I felt some risk in offering my truth. Along with two other members of SSUC, I shared something of our experience of being an affirming congregation with members of another congregation that is considering a journey into that explicit inclusivity. It is difficult to share the truth of my experience with those who wish to be affirmed in their thinking that it is enough for a church to simply say, "All are welcome." Some of us have experienced those words to be untruthful. It is difficult to speak one's truth when it is not what someone else wants to hear.

Another conversation that challenged my courage to speak my truth was with a journalist who wanted to interview me about a colleague in the United Church of Canada whose expression of her truth has led fellow clergy and members of the public to call for her resignation. As I expressed support for her truth and for her freedom to express it within the church, I wondered how my truth would be represented in print and what the backlash might be from those whose understandings differ from mine.

I spoke with another colleague who came to inquire about the expansive expression of the spirituality we are exploring in our community of faith. She was interested in how we are gathering with each other, what we are singing, how we welcome one another into community in celebrating rituals like baptism, how we understand prayer, and so on. It is difficult to speak one's truth to another who deeply values the more orthodox language, music, prayers, and rituals of the Christian tradition. It is challenging to share different truths without judgment, suspicion, or defensiveness.

It brought to mind for me an ancient story in the gospels about a nameless woman in a faceless crowd who found the courage to tell her truth. It is told as a miracle story, but I hear it as a parable. To most of that first century crowd, she was just another bloody woman. She bled to bring others into the world. She bled in rhythm with the cycles of the earth. She was an old woman, and she was still bleeding.

For a dozen years, the systems of healing had failed her. She tried everything, and nothing worked. Not wanting to cause a scene, not wanting to be seen, she came through the crowd and approached Jesus from behind to touch him. According to the storytellers, she only managed to touch his clothing.

The gospel writers treat her as an interruption, a bloody intrusion, a sideshow while Jesus is on his way to the main event – to help the dying daughter of an important man in the community. It would have taken great courage to show up and grasp at yet another straw. She must have feared one more disappointment. In her vulnerability, her character in the story teaches us something about the essential relationship between healing and truth.

She didn't escape detection. Despite the disciples' disinterest in her, the story tells us that Jesus needed to know her, speak with her, and hear her story. When she was singled out by Jesus in that crowd, she did something even more courageous – she told him all her truth. She went public with her pain.

What would she tell him? Would she tell him the painful truth of what it was like to be a woman in their culture, what it was like to be excluded by a religious tradition that made her untouchable? Would she tell him what it was like to be the object of their Levitical law that made her like a leper, contaminating anyone who would break the rules by being in her company, sitting where she sat, or doing the utterly unthinkable and actually touching her? Would she tell him what no first century man in their tradition would want to hear?

Would she tell him what it was like not to be hugged or held for more than a dozen years? Would she say how lonely she was, how isolated, how depressed, how many times she had tried to get help, but she just continued to hemorrhage? Would she tell him how many times she just wished she could die?

Would she tell him what it was like to be so alone, so afraid, so cut off from her family, her friends, and from the rituals and practices of her faith? Would she tell him about those who had blamed her for her bleeding, who made it her fault, who told her she was being punished for some secret sin she failed to confess? Would she speak about those who just didn't understand what it was to be so deeply wounded?

How long did it take for her to tell him all her truth? How did that truth change Jesus of Nazareth and change those who overheard it? How did their experience of such raw truth change the way they saw their society, their religion, and their role in perpetuating a system they didn't create?

The story gives us at least one hint. After hearing her truth, Jesus calls her "Daughter." He gives this unnamed woman a name. It had been a long time since she had been someone's daughter, and the one who now calls her "Daughter" is young enough to be her son. From the privileged place of his male gender in a patriarchal society, he names her as part of the human family, part of the family of faith in the tradition of ancient Judaism. He names her with respect as one who belongs, one who matters.

Healing doesn't generally happen unless our truth is heard and validated. This story offers me a teaching about the relationship between truth and healing rather than a miracle about disease and cure. Her experience of health is rooted in being freed and safe to speak her truth.

Sometimes truth is like vision that needs new lenses to correct it and give it focus. Placing it alongside the witness of other truths does this. Truth requires humility to recognize it is always partial and provisional. Our own truth is particular and subjective. It is the truth of our experience as we understand it and remember it that needs to be spoken and witnessed.

Truth is sometimes bloody, messy, and highly inconvenient. It often tells us things we would rather not know or pretend not to know. Yet only in the speaking and hearing of truth is there the deep possibility of healing.

Speaking truth is not a license to speak carelessly, unkindly, or aggressively. It is an invitation simply to speak softly and courageously, knowing what we speak is not *the* truth but *a* truth. It is *our* truth as we know it. Our hearts can hide in denial and be damaged by attempting to deceive ourselves and others. Or we can be opened toward healing by cultivating the habit of speaking truthfully. But let's not deceive ourselves – candor without kindness and compassion can hardly qualify as truth. But candor that has the courage to be faithful to its convictions *and* hear the convictions of another has the power to open the kind of healing space that was there between Jesus and a woman who came to be named "Daughter."

Our days bring new opportunities to practice this habit of the heart – to tell all our truth with humility, gentleness, and courage, and not be attached to the results. And as my annual practice attests in carrying forward these rules for living from one calendar to the next, it may be that we will always be in the process of forming habits. We come into each new moment with yet more experience and renewed intention to keep showing up, paying attention, telling the truth, and letting go of our grip on the results of our best efforts.

This reflection was offered on March 22, 2015.

The Practice of Creativity

Creativity, when all is said and done,
may be the best thing our species has going for it.

~ Matthew Fox ~
Creativity

They brought the colt to Jesus and threw their cloaks on it; and he sat on it. Many people spread their cloaks on the road, and others spread leafy branches that they had cut in the fields. Then those who went ahead and those who followed were shouting, "Hosanna! Blessed is the one who comes in the name of the Lord! Blessed is the coming kingdom of our ancestor David! ..." Mark 11:7-10

If we could imagine an episode of "This Hour Has 22 Minutes" when we read this first century story, I think we'd understand some of the wisdom it holds. We would see beyond the sweet, smiling, Sunday School Jesus, riding a donkey surrounded by some peasants staging a mock coronation. I think we'd see the cleverness of this performance art for what it is, if we could see the creativity that is at work here. It is a smart piece of street theatre premised on the truth that you can attract more flies with honey than with vinegar. You can expose more truth with humour than with force.

We domesticate this first century story when we make it pretty with waving palms and a red carpet of cloaks. We fail to see that what has come to town here is a highly political protest against what is broken in their society. Those who have made their way from Bethany with a borrowed donkey are enacting an alternative to military and imperial rule, an alternative to occupation, poverty, and oppression. Their performance piece is the result of advance planning to secure the necessary props, grassroots organizing to come together, walk together, and stand together against the corruption of temple practices and the complicity with a domination system.

Any community organizer would tell us that timing is everything. There was no coincidence about either the venue or the timing of this parody that was performed on the road from Bethany to Jerusalem. It was staged to capitalize on the peak season at the temple and high season in the city. It was the perfect opportunity to communicate a message not only to the Jewish religious leaders but also to their bedfellows, the Roman political leaders, who would all be in town because of Passover.

While the cleverly staged drama is entering the city from the east, no doubt the Roman military is marching in from the west, escorting the governor, Pilate, from his headquarters in Caesarea on the Mediterranean Sea. The crowd isn't lining the streets on the Mount of Olives but is gathered on the other side of town to watch Pilate ride his favourite war horse into town, flanked by legions of soldiers in military dress, all making their way to the palace. Each year at this time, Pilate, Caesar's highest ranking civil servant, comes to town so he can keep an eye on the throngs of pilgrims who have come to celebrate the Passover. His role is to enforce law and order, as the city swells with over 200,000 pilgrims in addition to its usual 40,000 residents. Any emperor is going to be a bit edgy as the pilgrims assemble to re-enact gaining their freedom from Pharaoh's repressive regime in Egypt generations before. It wouldn't take much for the crowd to make the leap from celebrating one liberation to seeking another.[16]

Unlike the main stage event, this fringe festival act doesn't go to Herod's palace where Pilate will stay while he's in town, or to the soldier's garrison – the home of the military power. The borrowed ass and its rider go straight to the temple. But Jesus and his friends don't exploit that stage by burning an effigy of Pilate or Caesar on the temple steps. There is no speech to rally the peasants into a confrontation with the military. Jesus doesn't try to stage a riot. He has brilliantly mocked the power of the empire and its religious collaborators without saying a word.

Jesus and his friends have staged this spoof to stand in solidarity with all those peasants who have been betrayed by their own leaders. It was also intended to offer angry resisters like the Zealots, who want to retaliate against Rome with force, a peaceful alternative to bring about social change. Over the next few days, those very peasants who ought to be protected by the institution of the temple will make a pilgrimage there to offer their sacrifice before celebrating the feast of Passover. They will be forced to pay temple tithes as well as Roman taxes and then ante up a little more again to line the pockets of the temple elite. Ironically, they will be forced to participate in this system of exploitation as they come to re-enact their liberation from an earlier domination system.

This clever piece of street theatre – riding a donkey into Jerusalem – demonstrates that there is no need to shout hatred or make death threats. This parody is long on symbolism with no need for a rant. The story recognizes that there is a time for persuasive speech, and there is a time for powerful symbolism. According to Mark's Jesus, careful planning, careful timing that captures the irony, a sense of humour, a farm animal, a few friends, and a good song have a better chance of stimulating change than throwing stones, drawing swords, firing guns, taking hostages, or dropping bombs.

This is an articulate critique of injustice without saying a word. It is an enactment of nonviolent resistance in a time that knows only too well that violence begets violence, and war does not make peace. This parody of coronation comes to the temple to say there is another way. Occupation does not lead to peace. Debt does not lead to peace. Co-opting the temple into the business of collecting taxes for Rome and giving away the peasants' land to the priests does not lead to peace. Turning the safe haven of the temple into a marketplace where forgiveness is sold and tribute is charged to line the pockets of the oppressor and the collaborator, does not lead to peace. There is no king like David to ride into town on his great white horse and give the people back their autonomy. Jesus' wordless message to the authorities is simple: what you are doing has all the ingredients necessary to breed generations of violence.

When this story was written, some 40 years or more after the death of Jesus, it was a time of great violence in Jerusalem. Perhaps the story was shaped as a script for resistance to inspire peaceful protest in the years of the Jewish revolt. Whether it is history remembered, or memory historicized, or a parable created about Jesus, it is a story calling for creativity during a terribly violent chapter of Jewish history, four decades after the execution of Jesus.

It is a story that invites us to engage our collective creativity to confront the deep injustices of our own time. It invites us to raise our protest at whatever temples of corruption and collusion oppress our most vulnerable citizens and against the policies and priorities that exploit the air, soil, and water upon which all life depends. Within this intriguing story is a call to expose, with satire and irony, the indefensibleness of exploitation in whatever form. It is a call to subvert power peacefully, embarrassing the emperors who are wearing clothes taken off someone's back.

Ours is a time that calls for unprecedented creativity. We need fewer soldiers and more artists. It is a time for imagination and ingenuity to expose injustice with a cleverness that disarms, like the fist in the velvet glove. We need a critique that can be delivered through satire, parody, poetry, stand-up comedy, theatre, or music.

If our creativity were to take to the streets, imagine the conversations we could provoke. Imagine the truths we might expose. Imagine the alternatives we might find to the terror and violence of our times.

Imagine what could happen if we were to look for donkeys, untie them, put them in the service of making an ass of what is, and offer a sign of what could be. Imagine what could happen if the powerful were to dismount their high horse and find the humility to hear what those who are protesting the violence of our society are trying to say. Where do we find the simple props and clever humour to demonstrate our "no" to injustice and follow it with the "yes" of another way?

Today's dissent has a way of becoming tomorrow's orthodoxy. No empire reigns forever. No theology or ideology holds all truth for all time. Change never comes through silence or complicity. Silence and collusion only serve to erode the soul. Truth demonstrated peacefully and creatively is our tool to expose and envision. Creativity is a habit of the heart. And it takes practice to keep discovering the life-enhancing possibilities that emerge when we place the power of our collective creativity in the service of our passion for a better way.

This reflection was offered on Palm Sunday,
March 29, 2015.

The Practice of Resilience

I die a thousand times
And am reborn another thousand ...

~ Julia Esquivel ~
"I Am Not Afraid of Death"

On the first day of the week, at early dawn, [the women] came to the tomb, taking the spices that they had prepared. They found the stone rolled away from the tomb, but when they went in, they did not find the body. While they were perplexed about this, suddenly two men in dazzling clothes stood beside them. The women were terrified and bowed their faces to the ground, but the men said to them, "Why do you look for the living among the dead? He is not here, but has risen." Luke 24:1-5

The turning of our planet toward its daystar is Earth's oldest ritual. The Easter story begins in the resilience of morning, in the great conspiracy of life to emerge through darkness into light. The story begins in the early morning because it is about the dawn of something new, a story that can only be set early in a new day and a new week, on the precipice of possibility.

This ancient story asks an ageless question, "Why do you look for the living among the dead?" If you have ever walked in old growth forest, you know there is no better place to look for the living than among the dead. This is the long witness of Earth. The things of death are always the conditions for life. Day comes out of night. Spring comes out of winter. Life grows out of the humus of what has gone before. The burial ground of the seed is the birthing ground of the flower. Nothing is wasted in nature; everything becomes something beyond itself. A scarred hillside charred with fire grows green with tender new shoots. The magnificent old growth forest is littered with nurse logs. The body of the fallen becomes the ground which nourishes the new generation that rises out of it. Energy is never lost. It just changes form.

In the world of the Easter tale, while the women did not find the body for which they had come, they found what they could never have imagined. Ironically, it is in those places which are soaked with long and deep memory that resilience begins. Our best hope of finding life after death is in the places alive with memory. The strangers at the tomb prompted the women to stop looking in the tomb and start searching the memory-laden places. "*Remember* what he told you while he was still in Galilee."[17]

Death had taken many things from them, but it had not robbed them of the power of memory. In the place where they had come to look for the dead, they not only recovered memory, but they also found new community. The strangers sent the women from the tomb to find the others, those who had not come with them that morning, those followers who were hiding in fear, those who were paralyzed by grief.

Though their leader had been cut down like a tree, memory became a nurse log that birthed a new and living community. Memory became the humus which seeded a community that would grow into a forest. In looking for the one who was their *tree,* they became a *forest.* No longer would their dreams for their people and their world reside in an individual but rather in the power of the collective – in each of them and all of them together. It would reside in those of us, generations later, in whom the power of the vision Jesus seeded is planted.

Resurrection was the name they gave to their experience of transformation. While they did not find his body, they found within themselves that which they had never lost. The empire had killed their teacher but not his teaching. The empire had only buried his body but not their vision for a new earth community.

These Easter stories are not about what happened to the corpse of Jesus. They are about what happened to the community of Jesus. They are not stories about the resuscitation of a body but of the resilience of the human spirit and the capacity to seed a new community. It is about how the community that was connected to Jesus in life rose up after his death, like new growth rising out of an ancient forest.

Easter is the name our ancients gave to the god of fertility. Easter is our name for the experiences we have of awakening to the regenerative nature of life. Easter is every experience we have of finding the living among the dead, finding hope in the ashes of despair, and finding possibility in places that reek with impossibility. These are the places where endings are just beginnings backward. On Easter day we celebrate the miracle of becoming a community that empowers each new generation to find what is living amid what is dying and to nurture that life. It is the spiritual practice of resilience.

This reflection was offered on Easter Sunday, April 5, 2015.

The Practice of Communion

*We are participants in a vast communion of being,
and if we open ourselves to its guidance,
we can learn anew how to live in this great
and gracious community of truth.*

~ Parker Palmer ~
Let Your Life Speak

Simon Peter said to [the others], "I am going fishing." They said to him, "We will go with you." They went out and got into the boat, but that night they caught nothing. Just after daybreak, Jesus stood on the beach; but the disciples did not know that it was Jesus. Jesus said to them, "Children, you have no fish, have you?" They answered him, "No." He said to them, "Cast the net to the right side of the boat, and you will find some." So they cast it, and now they were not able to haul it in because there were so many fish. John 21:3-6

When I was on sabbatical in 2010, my spouse, Dawn, and I spent a lot of time walking the headlands above the Pacific Ocean on the northern coast of California. On one of those walks, we were joined by our friend, Diane. She was terminally ill at the time and would die two years later. On that day, among the many wonders we witnessed, we spent time in the company of a magnificent flock of pelicans. Diane was captivated by them and comforted by their presence, as she navigated her way toward her death, seeking to live each day as deeply and fully as she could.

Last summer, we walked that trail again. When we returned to the beach below the village, a lone pelican appeared above us and perched on a rock. We felt as though we were in Diane's presence once again, transported back to the beauty and wonder we had shared with her years earlier. We found ourselves remembering the gifts of that day and the little bit of heaven we all experienced together in the company of those comical and graceful creatures, playing in the updraft just above the breaking waves.

We can never underestimate the power of place to evoke memory and presence. For the community of Jesus, Galilee was the place that was soaked with memory. It was on the hillsides, in the villages, and on the shores of the Galilee that fishermen, villagers, labourers – Palestinian peasants – formed a new community inspired by the teachings of Jesus of Nazareth. In those places around the Galilee, he had instilled a hope in his followers that the "kingdom of God" would displace the tyrannical rule of Rome. It isn't surprising that each of the first century gospel writers are intent on returning the friends of Jesus to the Galilee after his death. It is the place where memory has the best chance of inspiring the movement that will take them into the future.

Their return to those shores is a shift from the heartbreak that happened in Jerusalem to a place where they can replay, rework, and *re-member* the memories that can best be recovered in the Galilee. We can picture these first century disciples looking for a bit of comfort and hope along those familiar shores. We recognize that moment when Peter says, "I am going fishing," as the moment when we each walk through a door in our grief to the place when the grip of sadness loosens its hold on us a little.

For Peter, this was the first step toward getting on with life, after the death of someone he loved. It was a step into the serenity that comes in resuming a familiar routine, returning to the work he knew best. This was not about finding distractions to help him detour around his grief. He was not a recreational fisherman. It was not a day of rest and relaxation, of catch and release. It was a going back to the place where he first met Jesus, the place where he had begun a journey that seemed to have ended in Jerusalem. It was a return to the place where he was forever changed.

The storyteller is right to have his friends say, "We will go with you." We need those people who will go with us. We need the company of those who won't say, "I know just how you feel" or, "You'll get over it" or, "You've grieved long enough, it's time to get on with your life." We need those people who will walk with us through the sadness into the storied places of our lives, as we touch our memories and start to stir into life again.

It is an unusual fishing story. There was no big one that got away. There was a night of failure, of empty nets. But when morning came, the next chapter of life dawned with the memory of the one who had called them from their nets on this very shore a few years earlier. In this place, Jesus had invited them to put out into the deep and cast their nets on the port side of their boat. There was the memory of the deep hope that filled their empty nets. They were compelled by his vision for life and the potential he saw for human community. The experience of those years with their teacher and with one another didn't allow them to simply return to fishing. They were no longer fishermen. They had become community organizers, visionaries who would nourish the dream of those who were hungry for more than fish and bread, more than subsistence and survival.

In their communion with a storied place and with one another, they began to discern that the familiar presence, now absent in their aching hearts, could still be found along the ambiguous shore between uncertain ground and familiar waters. That sense of presence returns in the places where memory helps all of us navigate the uncertain future, where our experiences of a little bit of heaven bring us right back to earth, where our communion with the past propels us to take up residence in the present in a new and more intentional way.

These stories the first century writers give us are not ghost stories. They are not stories of a dead man walking the beach and making breakfast, just as my story of Diane is not a story of her returning reincarnated as a pelican. These are stories of our deep communion with life and the sacred presence that calls us back to life from the depths of disappointment and despair. They are stories that help us live after death, to find life after grief, to be forever changed by our communion with the ones we love in this life.

These are the stories of *our own* resurrections, of our coming back to life after the death of a particular role in our lives, a relationship, a job, a vocation, a career, an identity, a way of understanding our faith or making meaning of our lives, a disaster, a death of someone we love, a devastating disappointment. These are the tales of our rising into life again in the great communion with all that has gone before us. It takes practice to be open to the wisdom of memory. It is a habit of the heart to train our eyes to look within ourselves and in one another to see the sacred presence we call by so many different names.

We recognize ourselves in Peter and his friends in this ancient story. They found the presence of the absent one in returning to the places they had shared together. In the midst of our grief, may we open to the deep connection of place and memory to hear the ways we are called back to life, forever changed by our communion with all that goes before us.

This reflection was offered on April 12, 2015.

The Practice of Hope

The very least you can do in your life is to figure out what you hope for. And the most you can do is live inside that hope. Not admire it from a distance but live right in it, under its roof.

~ Barbara Kingsolver ~
Animal Dreams

Faith is the assurance of things hoped for, the conviction of things not seen. Hebrews 11:1

Hope is hard. It is especially hard near the end of a lifetime, when hope asks us to have the vision to see beyond our own mortality and place our hope in those who will go beyond us. I think that's why these words of Jack Layton, in a letter to Canadians a few days before he died, say so much to me: "My friends, love is better than anger. Hope is better than fear. Optimism is better than despair. So let us be loving, hopeful, and optimistic. And we'll change the world."[18]

I am struck by his engagement with life on his deathbed and the collective identity this farewell message embraces from one who knows that he will have no further opportunity to change the world. But even as his own death draws near, he sees that in acts of love, hope, and optimism, he will be part of the "we" that can change the world. It is not a mere passing of the torch to those who will survive him, but a real sense of being a participant in the changes to the world that will come after him. That is what is instructive to me about hope.

Hope is a way of both seeing the world as it is and seeing the world we long for. It requires seeing ourselves as part of a much larger whole than what is represented by our singular lifetime. Hope is a way of seeing that has a long sense of story, a wide sense of ourselves, and a deep sense of time. It requires an identity that is more than the personal, a sense of belonging to a family, a community, a nation, a planet.

Many of the characters the biblical narratives give us were really good at this. We are instructed by those who gave themselves to dreams that they would never live to see become reality. For instance, take the great patriarch, Abraham, and the model matriarch, Sarah. They leave a settled life in Haran to pursue the dream of founding a great nation and a great people. For most of their lifetime, however, they lack the two things necessary to establish a great nation. They have neither a host of descendants nor a territory of land which they can pass on.

By the time death claims them, Abraham has managed to father only two sons, each by a different mother. They are half-brothers who continue the Genesis tradition of deadly sibling competition and combat, two sons who have no common dream and no shared hope, even in the wake of their father's death. Yet three major world religions trace their origin to Abraham. Two major tribal identities, Jews and Arabs, trace their lineage back to him.

Abraham's line includes another legendary giant among biblical characters, namely Moses. He is a reluctant leader who manages to start a guided trek from enslavement to freedom. Against great odds, he becomes the liberator of the Hebrews oppressed in Egypt. Although he succeeds in freeing them from slavery, the story doesn't reward him with arriving at the destination of freedom. As his life ends, he sees the land he has been walking toward for years, but he never gets to cross the Jordan River and celebrate having completed the journey with what became a rebellious and disbelieving band of followers. He didn't live to see the national identity he inspired. He didn't live to be recognized for his leadership.

In the book of Hebrews, in the Christian Scriptures, there is a chapter that reads like that sidewalk in Hollywood that features the names of the greatest stars in the entertainment industry. In the 11th chapter of Hebrews, we find the sidewalk of names of many of the shining stars in the stories that shape our faith tradition. Abraham and Sarah get a star in that sidewalk because they kept living into a hope that wouldn't be realized in their lifetime. Moses gets a star in that sidewalk because he was faithful to the vision of freedom, even though he wouldn't get to taste it fully himself.

History has given us many mentors in hope. Gandhi and many of those who marched to the sea with him merely glimpsed the independence of India for which they worked most of their adult life. Gandhi inspired its vision, though he didn't live long within it. Martin Luther King Jr. and Rosa Parks didn't live to see a desegregated nation, a nation that would be led by a Black man in their children's lifetime. This is what hope looks like. It has a long view of time and a large view of the part we play by virtue of having been born. Hope is far-sighted.

We could say that all of these lived in more hopeful times than we do, but we know that hope was no easier then than it is now. We see outcomes they could scarcely imagine. It is not that the lives of earlier generations were easier than ours – we see with the eyes of hindsight. Hope requires no more and no less of us than it has of all who have gone before and all who will come after us.

Hope needs certain conditions to survive. Hope thrives when we live in the larger story of who we are. Indigenous peoples instruct us well in nurturing our self-understanding – that we are part of a cosmic network of relationships of those gone before us and our children who will come after us. We are part of an *eco system* rather than an *ego system*.[19] We are one creature among the many who make their lives on this planetary home.

Hope has the humility to remember that while life is about four billion years old, human life is less than a quarter of a million years old. It doesn't measure success or progress in three-month probations or five-year plans. Hope is rooted in a long view of time that trusts the cumulative power of each of us doing what we can, while we can, with our sight focussed on the life that will go beyond us. Each of us is like a cell in a larger organism with a role to play in a hopeful tomorrow.

The power of the Jesus movement has always been in knowing that its vision is bigger than any one person. That vision did not die when its leader was executed in the first century, because it was planted and rooted in a community. As those early movement builders discovered, "we are the ones we have been waiting for."[20] This is not an arrogant self-understanding. It is an essential responsibility for participating in the culture we long for someone to create – the world we hope to pass on to our children and their children.

Anger, fear, and despair have tempted every generation. They are easy options that forever fail the future. Hope doesn't just spring eternal. It is cultivated as a habit of the heart. It isn't self-seeding. Hope is nurtured by seeing the big picture of our brief human place in a multiverse that has found its way through many a crisis with unimaginable creativity. Hope holds a long and deep view of time.

As cosmic citizens, we make our home on a planet possessed of creative energies that have found an inventive way forward. As Jews, Christians, and Muslims, we are rooted in a common faith that has always looked beyond a single lifetime. It is a faith that sees clearly how things are yet refuses to give up hope that something better is possible. We keep building the muscle of hope in the long, deep, and wide story of life, planting small seeds of possibility.

This reflection was offered on April 19, 2015, in celebration of Earth Day.

The Practice of Wonder

Wonder will guide us.

~ Brian Swimme ~
Journey of the Universe

The disciples came to Jesus and asked, "Who is the greatest in the kingdom of heaven?" He called a child, whom he put among them, and said, "Truly I tell you, unless you change and become like children, you will never enter the kingdom of heaven." Matthew 18:1-3

We see it so clearly in our newest arrivals. Once our eyes begin to adjust to the light and we recover our equilibrium from the journey out of warmth and darkness and the music of our mother's heart, we soon become enchanted with everything. Our eyes follow movement and fix upon whatever sparkles or shines. Sounds command our attention. Our fingers and toes are fascinating enough to fit into our mouths to taste.

When we do get to our feet, it takes forever to go anywhere because everything is worth stopping for. Every little stone or shell or weed is worthy of picking for presents, and dandelions are as beautiful as any rose will ever be. Cardboard boxes can become a castle and wonders never cease.

When we discover words, *why* becomes one of our favourites. It quickly becomes a great irritant to adults who have stopped asking *why* or saying *wow* and are no longer amazed by all the sacred altars that litter our world. What happened to all that wonder we arrive with? Where does it go? How do we propose to live without it? What does it take for us to be astonished now?

Our loss of wonder is dangerous, maybe even deadly – deadly to our relationship with Earth and with each other, and dangerous to our relationship with all that is sacred. As a species, our wonder has led us to some amazing insights and inventions. Asking *why* has changed the ways we understand our world and how we relate to the soil and air. It has changed the ways we feed ourselves and the ways we live in relationship with other creatures on our planet. Our sense of wonder has taken us to the moon and back and led us to insights about how life stirred and evolved in this special place we call home.

Wonder moved our ancestors to a deep sense of reverence for sun and moon, tides and seasons, wind and rain. It is a reverence we are quick to call primitive or superstitious, a reverence that we have lost to our so-called enlightenment. There is a great irony in this. As we moved from the industrial revolution into today's technical revolution, our sense of wonder seems to have diminished in direct proportion to finding ourselves with greater powers to alter life on this planet.

The loss of wonder has put us and our planet in great peril. We are not talking about an environmental crisis here; we are talking about a spiritual one. It is the kind of crisis the friends of Jesus were warned about in the first century. We live in a time when we are in danger of gaining the whole world and losing our own soul,[21] of gaining power over all that makes life possible on this planet and losing what makes us truly alive, what makes us human. It is perilous for we who are spiritual beings in a human experience.

Rabbi Abraham Heschel, a great Jewish teacher of the twentieth century, is credited with the insight that to be spiritual is to be amazed.[22] Isn't this the wisdom we are re-learning from science in the new universe story?[23] Isn't this the spiritual wisdom the first century writers attribute to the teachings of Jesus? Matthew's Jesus gives us the insight about needing to become like little children to enter the kingdom of heaven. What is the enduring wisdom for our species in this teaching? Is it not a way of inviting us to recover our soul by becoming children of wonder?

In the language of our first century teacher and prophet, unless we become like children – unless we recover and return to our essential humanity, to the essence of what it is to be spirit in human form – we will cease to be human. Unless we adopt the innocence and humility of a child, our humanity is in great peril as is everything on this planet.

Wonder inoculates us against the arrogance that leads us to think we are the apex of creation, uniquely made in the image of the divine to dominate and manage all the so-called lesser and lower forms of life. Wonder will teach us that we did not emerge in evolutionary wisdom to be king of the hill. We emerge onto the hill, carrying the wisdom of all that came before us, totally dependent on the ever-evolving wisdom of everything that is, or was, or ever will be on this hill with us. Perhaps it is only wonder that will guide us into a new relationship with our planet, with ourselves, and with all that is sacred.

Isn't this the spiritual wisdom our indigenous brothers and sisters have treasured in the teachings of their elders? It is the spiritual practice of wonder that invites us to know every rock and leaf, every mountain and sea, every raven and rabbit as "all my relations,"[24] as cousins and kin, as sparks of divine light, as essential partners in life.

Perhaps if we never got over the miracle of being born, we would live as children of wonder. We would know that we are not the top of the totem, king of the castle, apex of creation, or even the universe come to consciousness, but humus in human form, stardust in human form. We are composed of the same elements as every other living thing, carrying forward within us every evolutionary experiment that happened before now. We are one of many cousins and kin, creatures of the cosmos, born to be children of awe and wonder, no more and no less.

Whether we arrive in this world into the arms of two people longing to be parents or are here as an unexpected oops, our birth delivered us into this world in this particular form with this specific genetic makeup against astronomical odds. We're talking miracle here! It is not some miracle of design but the greater miracle of chance and circumstance – like the miracle of supernovas exploding, birthing a planet that would be just the right distance from the sun, the goldilocks of the galaxy. Here we are on this wild and precious planet that is neither too hot nor too cold with just the right conditions for hydrogen and oxygen to mate into water in which living organisms could incubate, a planet with just enough warmth and enough light from the sun for life to evolve.

Consider the odds of any of us being here. What are the chances of two people coupling at just the right moment for the one possible sperm to fertilize the one possible egg that would result in you or me? I'd guess the odds were something like a million to one against you being you and me being me or either of us being here at all, let alone being here at the same time in the same place.

That's just the beginning of the miracle. The same unlikely happenstance had to repeat itself for generations, not only in all our human ancestors but also in all our more than human ones as well. Our birth hinges on an almost infinite sequence of happenings against great odds.[25]

If we were never to get over the miracle of getting here, we might live with the kind of wonder and humility that would keep us human and keep us from harming or destroying any form of life, let alone fouling our nest and endangering our planet. Surely the time has come to hear with new ears the first century wisdom that invites us to be a new kind of planetary presence and to build a new *kin-dom* which has the power to make our earth the heaven of our dreams. To cure what ails us requires returning a sense of wonder to our species. It is to be like the child Jesus celebrated in the story – open and trusting, curious and enchanted, dependent and vulnerable, humble and hopeful.

Were we to see our humanity as one humble expression of humus, wouldn't we come down off the hill, bow in reverence before the first thing we meet, and sing our gratitude for the gift of life? Then we would find a way to be about the work of shrinking our footprint and our market share, protecting our air and water, and using our big brains and large hearts to find a way to be one with creation.

To not lose our innate sense of wonder takes practice. The wonder that keeps us humble is a habit of the heart, a spiritual practice to cultivate. What wonder might be just waiting for you to notice?

This reflection was offered on April 26, 2015.

The Practice of Letting Go

*Knowledge is learning something new every day.
Wisdom is letting go of something every day.*

~ Zen Proverb ~

Now there was a Pharisee, a respected religious scholar named Nicodemus, a leader among the Jewish people. He came to Jesus under the cover of darkness and said to him, "Rabbi, we know that you are a teacher who has come from the great and holy Oneness; for no one can do what you do unless they are in touch with the depths of that sacredness." Jesus answered him, "Truly, I tell you, no one can experience the realm of the sacred without being born again." Nicodemus said to him, "How can anyone be reborn after having grown old? Can one enter a second time into the mother's womb and be born?" And Jesus answered him, "Don't be surprised when I say that you must be born again and again." Paraphrase of John 3:1-4

During our annual garage sale, the church building is jammed full of things we are ready to shed. It is stuff from our garages, basements, and closets that we were once attached to or thought we needed. It's clothing we wore occasionally or things we thought we might have a use for someday. Whatever our reason for getting it in the first place, its grip on us has loosened and we are ready to let it go. Perhaps there is a spiritual truth to be learned from a garage sale.

It is the same life lesson that a first century writer gave us. Written some 60 years after the execution of Jesus, the gospel of John introduces a conversation between Jesus and Nicodemus, a religious leader in first century Judaism. Perhaps this conversation was constructed as a teaching device for the early followers of the way of Jesus. It is a story that tells us something about how those spiritual seekers were emerging from their Jewish roots and forging a new identity as followers of the teachings of Jesus. In finding their new way, they were struggling with both letting go and holding on to the tradition out of which their movement was born.

The writer of John's gospel casts Nicodemus, a member of the Pharisees, as a conversation partner for Jesus. Pharisees were the guardians of first century Judaism. They were the religious leaders their people looked to for all the answers. But Nicodemus appears to be afraid of his own questions.

He was very hesitant to risk letting go of rabbinically defined religion to explore a more porous spirituality, even though it intrigued him. Being a respected religious scholar entrusted with preserving the ancient traditions of his faith, it would not do for Nicodemus to be seen in broad daylight, having a conversation with this non-credentialed, rural mystic. So the writer sets this luminous conversation under the cover of darkness.

Perhaps we are hearing a conversation that was occurring at the time this story was written. It was the strained conversation between those Jews who had been expelled from the synagogue (because they were following the expansive way they learned in the teachings of Jesus) and those Jews who remained loyal to the Judaism of the synagogue after the destruction of the temple in Jerusalem in 70 CE.

Isn't this conversation representative of a classic collision of mindsets? As we listen in, we realize that Nicodemus and Jesus don't speak the same language. This is a brave attempt at dialogue between a mystic and a literalist, between one possessed of a spirituality shaped by letting go and another who is possessed of a religion defined by its adherence to a fixed tradition.

If we think of this story as a parable rather than an historical memory, we might hear a perennial lesson from the curriculum of every enduring wisdom tradition. To be fully and deeply alive, to be in touch with our deepest identity as a human being/a human becoming, we must be newly born to each new day. "How can this be?" Nicodemus asked.

He was stumped by the image of trying to squeeze himself back into his mother's womb. It was hard enough just getting off a donkey these days. Here we have an affluent intellectual, a member of the ruling council, who wouldn't know a metaphor if it was staring him in the eye.

Nicodemus couldn't let go of his literal, linear, logical mind to grasp the metaphor before him. Jesus told him that if he wanted to engage a spiritual life, he had to awaken to the mystery of birth. He had to awaken to the utterly repeatable experience of being born – being delivered from the womb of security in which he had taken refuge, from the womb of answers to questions no one was even asking anymore, from the womb of authority which required living inside the shelter of his received laws, traditions, and practices. He had made a palace out of his answers that were, at best, intended to be as provisional as a tent. To be most truly alive, he had to give himself to the process of birth, trusting the dark passage that opens into the ambiguous, messy reality of being fully alive.

To live life as a spiritually awake human being requires each of us to leave the womb of our present attachments. To be born again is to let go of our closely guarded ideas, our treasured beliefs, and give ourselves to the vulnerable journey of opening to the mystery in which we live. It is about awakening to a universe saturated with the spiritual, infused with the sacred, intimately divine, and intensely holy. It is about being newly born every morning and growing more deeply conscious as a spiritual being with each new day.

It is about the birthing of consciousness, the awakening of spirit that comes from the kind of openness that allows oneself to be as though newly born to each new moment, each new day, relationship, and experience. To be born again is to be ever a newborn, meeting the world with wonder, filled with awe and mystery, inviting discovery, requiring faith and trust. It is by letting go that we are born again and again. It is by letting go that we live.

Birth is our first opportunity to begin to learn the spiritual practice of letting go. We learn that life is about leaving one place for another, one stage of life for another, one understanding for another. We learn to loosen our grip and go with the flow of life's river.

Life both begins and ends with letting go. Birth is possible only by letting go of our cramped, wet quarters of warmth and darkness. It is not a letting go we are quick to choose. Our small bodies are pushed out of the comfort to which they cling and squeezed with great resistance through a narrow passage into a lifetime of both embracing and letting go.

Death, too, requires a letting go, a letting go of what was, what is, and what might have been. In death, we let go of what is seen and what we know to embrace a becoming beyond our dependence on breath. Every moment between birth and death is about holding loosely the fragile threads with which our lives are woven.

Everything I have learned about letting go, I've learned from my elders. In the grief of leaving my first pastoral relationship, I recognized that the parishioner who was most able to say goodbye was the one who had lived the longest and had the most practice in letting go. She was by far the eldest member of that congregation and had lived almost three and a half times longer than I had lived. I was struck by the way she freed me to go on, and I could see how practiced she was in letting life come and letting it go.

The long-widowed women of Buchanan Eastwood United Church, with whom I shared spiritual community for five years, taught me that life requires us to loosen our grip – like the trapeze artist who must let go of the bar or the hands of another to continue the graceful gesture of an aerialist routine. I admired the wisdom of those who determined when it was time to let go of driving their cars, let go of the pain of surviving their spouses and often the loss of their children, and live with gratitude, accepting what is and what will be.

It takes a lifetime of practice to learn to let go: to let go of stimulation and surrender to sleep; to let go of our parent's hand and walk on our own; to let go of each stage of life – our infancy, childhood, adolescence, middle essence, and even our elderhood.

For in letting go of life, we find more of it. By letting go of this moment, we are born anew into the next.

It seems to me this is the essence of the teaching in the conversation between Jesus and Nicodemus. To walk the wisdom of Jesus is to embrace a life of letting go – where everyday is our *birth day* – a day into which we are invited to be newly born. As we practice the spiritual discipline of letting go, let's begin by asking ourselves where we need to release our hold and trust that life will carry us safely beyond our grip to live in the ways that seek birth at every opportunity.

This reflection was offered on May 3, 2015.

The Practice of Deepening

I will not die an unlived life.
I will not live in fear
of falling or catching fire.
I choose to inhabit my days,
to allow my living to open me,
to make me less afraid,
more accessible,
to loosen my heart
until it becomes a wing,
a torch, a promise.
I choose to risk my significance;
to live so that which came to me as seed
goes to the next as blossom
and that which came to me as blossom,
goes on as fruit.[26]

~ Dawna Markova ~

[Jesus] said to Simon, "Put out into the deep water and let down your nets for a catch." Simon answered, "Master, we have worked all night long but have caught nothing. Yet if you say so, I will let down the nets." When they had done this, they caught so many fish that their nets were beginning to break. Luke 5:4-6

I love to be *at* the water. I like to be *on* the water. But I am most reluctant to be *in* the water. That's an embarrassing admission for a Maritimer to make, but it's true. I prefer to sit at the edge of the pool rather than make my way into the deep end. I like to wade at the shore and avoid getting anything more than my ankles wet.

On a few rare occasions, I've been persuaded to venture into deeper waters. The first time I ever snorkelled was easy. It was that Hawaii kind of snorkelling where you put your face in the water, keep your feet on the ground, and sunburn your derriere, while seeing a few amazing things.

But twice in my life, my much more adventurous spouse has managed to get me into deeper waters. On our first trip to the Middle East, Dawn persuaded me to snorkel in the Red Sea at the edge of a coral reef – a place the local Bedouin called "The Blue Hole." It might have been a blue hole to the locals, but it was a black hole to me. I experienced a wave of panic that washed over me when my body floated beyond the reef where you couldn't begin to see the bottom, let alone touch bottom.

Six years later, in the ocean waters of the Atlantic off the coast of St. Croix in the U.S. Virgin Islands, we experienced an even more adventurous kind of snorkelling. You sail for an hour, jump off the boat into the waves weighted down by your fins, and force yourself to swim out to the reef. Once again, there were some truly spectacular things to see, things you would never see by staying on the shore or sights you couldn't experience without taking to the deep water. And the amazingly diverse and colourful sea life made it worth facing down my fears and swimming over the reef to the ledge where it seemed like the bottom dropped right out of the sea. I felt like I was looking right into the face of the deep.

Although snorkelling has only called me out into the deep waters a few times in my life, I have discovered that life calls us into deep waters every day. Beyond the superficial conversations we have about the weather, the guarded ways we tell each other what we think and feel, beyond our ideas and our opinions, life invites us again and again to put out into the deep. In the conversations we have about meaning, about the universe, about purpose and destiny, about life and death, about our hopes and fears, we set out into the deep. Deep wells of emotion spring up that bring moments of beauty and seasons of loss. We explore the deep relationships we have with one another, with Earth our home, and with the other expressions of life with which we share this planet.

There is a story, shared by the writer of the Gospel of Luke, where Jesus invites Simon to "put out into the deep water." The wisdom teacher invites his friend to put himself in a place we all fear. We are more than a little afraid of the deep questions, deepest emotions, deep encounters, deep experiences, the deep places. Most of us are afraid, in some way, of putting out into the deep.

We fear going under or being overwhelmed by life's depth. We are afraid of our own deep places. Simon answered for all of us when he said, "Come on, we've been there half the night and we've caught nothing except our death of cold." When we drop our guard, let down our defences, bare our souls, unshield our hearts, it's just too scary.

To be fully alive is to know the trouble and beauty of life's deepest places, whether it is with Jesus in the Jordan, Buddha under the Bodhi tree, Moses in Midian, Isaiah in the temple, Simon on the sea, Matthew leaving his desk job, Mary weeping in the garden, or our own vows of baptism to live with open hearts. The invitation of the spiritual life is a call to "put out into the deep." It is an invitation to engage the depths of mystery, to sink into the sacredness of life's terror and beauty, to sink into the deep holiness of life and death – willing to resist the superficial, to refuse to be satisfied with slogans or creeds or certainty. To put out into the deep is a way to not die an unlived life. It is to inhabit each of our days, to allow our living to open us, to be less afraid and more accessible, to loosen our hearts until they become a wing.[27]

Where the deep calls, fear inevitably answers. To put out into the deep in the company of our fear is to find ourselves in the depths of life and to know there is no place we can ever go where we will not be at home in the universe. To sink into the sacred is to be immersed in the grace of life, to discover that just past our fear is the abundance and wonder of the deep.

When we swim beyond the warm, shallow waters, willing to go below the surface, we deepen our joys and our sorrows, deepen our humanity, deepen our experience of life and death. We deepen our engagement with life. And it takes practice to go deeper. This is a time to ask ourselves where life is calling us into the deep just now.

This reflection was offered on May 10, 2015.

The Practice of Pausing

There is more to life than increasing its speed.
~ Mahatma Gandhi ~

Observe the sabbath day and keep it holy ... Six days you shall labour and do all your work. But the seventh day ... you shall not do any work ... Deuteronomy 5:12-14

For several years, I have attended an annual preaching conference. It is a perverse kind of Sabbath for preachers to sit in uncomfortable and crowded pews with 1,800 others to listen to speaker after speaker offer their best sermons. It always restores my appreciation for what it is to be a listener! There comes a point, as every good audience knows, when the butt has reached its capacity for listening. So I punctuate those conference days with a leisurely read of the daily news, an unhurried walk, and people watching on downtown streets. Then there is the inevitable critique of the daily sermons with colleagues, each of us grateful to have been in a pew instead of the pulpit.

Whenever I turned on the television or picked up a newspaper in Denver during the most recent preaching conference, the headline news was about a train crash in Pennsylvania. It wasn't long before the cause of that crash was attributed to the train moving at twice the posted speed on a particular curve of track. Seven deaths and over 200 injuries were caused by excessive speed.

It took less than 24 hours for that news story to cease to be about the tragic loss of lives. The focus soon shifted to how so many commuters were going to get to work in New York City with this disruption of rail service on that busy stretch of track. We couldn't pause very long in the shadow of death before turning our minds to the self-serving concerns of surviving commuters. The story quickly centred on the inconvenience this accident caused in a culture addicted to expediency and efficiency, in a culture addicted to speed.

In downtown Denver, I observed power lunches and people rushing between office buildings, conducting "confidential" conversations on cell phones along crowded sidewalks as they dashed to the next appointment. I listened to my colleagues catching up on a year's happenings since we last saw one another. When we ask how the past year was, everyone's answer is always the same. "It was busy!" Who would we be if we were not busy?

Some time ago, I read that in China the polite answer to the question, "How are you?" is "I am very busy, thank you." If you are busy, then the assumption is you must be fine. If you have more to do than you can do, and the list never gets done but only gets longer, then you must be *very* fine.[28]

What is this love affair we have with busyness? What is this compulsion to see what needs to be done as endless, and this aversion to spending time in ways that appear to accomplish nothing? Why is leisure so exceptional that we must leave home or get sick for it to happen?

Maybe that's why each of the enduring religious traditions of our world invites us to pause from production and consumption. They teach us how to be spiritual beings by listening to our hearts, listening to a rhythm that is, like music, a conversation between sound and silence.

Buddhism teaches us the meditative and contemplative pauses that give our minds a rest. It offers practices that invite us to be filled with the present moment, as we empty our hands and our hearts. We learn a stillness that helps us to let go of the cravings and desires that drive our lives into mindless living.

For our Jewish cousins, the practice of Sabbath is the pause that refreshes. After six days of playing "beat the clock" comes a seventh day to "stop the clock." It is a day unlike the others – a day to pause from the great work of building the world and tend to the holy work of caring for the soul. The Sabbath is a practice prescribed in Exodus, Leviticus, and Deuteronomy, three ancient books of instruction. It's a practice designed to keep production and consumption in some kind of sustainable balance and keep a health-giving rhythm between work and rest. There is a time to build and a time to behold, a time to create and a time to stand back in appreciation. The Sabbath is a pause in the cycle of production. It is a time to rest as though all the work that needed doing had been done in the previous six days.

Imagine hitting a pause button and acting like everything that needs to be done is done and there is nothing left on the to-do list. Imagine stopping for 24 hours and acting like there is nothing more important than to light a candle and say a prayer, watch the sunset, linger over a good meal, sleep without setting an alarm clock, gather with friends to sing and pray, or walk nowhere in particular. It is not walking to raise our heart rate but to notice every smell, colour, creature, and texture. There is something healing that comes from pausing to appreciate what is around you and giving thanks when the sun sets on this perfect day. When you step back into the rhythm of production and consumption for another six days, you do so with renewed energy and sense of purpose.

In the Jewish tradition, the Sabbath pause was a way to ensure rest for the animals and the land, for every being and everything that we put to work. It isn't just about us. Perhaps it isn't even primarily for the wellbeing of the human creature. After six years of faithful service, debts were to be forgiven, slaves freed, and property restored to those who had lost it. For everything and everyone it was a rebalancing and a fresh start.

Our planet needs a Sabbath too – a pause when we are neither taking from it nor giving it more to deal with than it can handle. Imagine what a difference it would make if Earth got one day off every week, free from emissions, pollutants, mining, fishing, and the demands we make for the sake of our production and consumption.

Christianity remodelled the Sabbath practice into a day of resurrection, a pause on the first day of the week that celebrates coming back to life again. Islam reframes the Sabbath, punctuating each day with five pauses for prayer – five invitations to stop working, eating, or sleeping in order to be mindful of who we are and how we have been blessed.

Something in each religious tradition has tuned into the truth about the human spirit. We need time to pause, reflect, wonder, and re-orient ourselves in time. Even the mechanics of our heart tell us that a healthy rhythm requires a pause between the beats. Our ears tell us that music that moves our feet to dance is made with patterns of sound and silence. It takes both notes and rests to create the rhythm that moves our spirits to sing. The cycles of the natural world have a built-in rhythm with a season to plant, a season to tend, a season to harvest, and a season to let the field lie fallow and rest.

The invitation is with us each day: "Oh, do you have time / to linger / for just a little while / out of your busy // and very important day / ... it is a serious thing // just to be alive / on this fresh morning / in this broken world ..."[29] This is our moment to create a new relationship with time, to make a commitment to hit the pause button and cultivate a Sabbath practice that refreshes and renews us and all those around us.

*This reflection was offered on May 17, 2015, on the
Victoria Day Weekend, the first long weekend of the summer season.*

The Practice of Singing

Anything worth thinking about is worth singing about.

~ Bob Dylan ~
The Essential Interviews

Let the heavens be glad, and let the earth rejoice;
let the sea roar, and all that fills it;
let the field exult and everything in it.
Then shall all the trees of the forest sing for joy.

Psalm 96:11-12

I can't imagine a world without music. One of the things I love about spring is the symphony I wake to each morning. At our home in South Cooking Lake, songbirds start the music earlier and earlier with the growing light. Their voices are joined by ducks, gulls, and geese, and before long, it is the chorus of ravens and squirrels that carry the song. It is up to the red-winged blackbird to usher in the night.

Each new day, the natural world, one of the great spiritual teachers, is at work, teaching us to sing, whether we can carry a tune or not. Whether we have been told we have a lovely voice, or we've been invited only to sing in the shower because we can't carry a tune in a bucket, we all sing. Whether we ever open our mouths or match our voices to those little birds perched on the wires of lines and spaces on a treble or bass staff, we all sing,

Irrespective of what our voice does or does not do, we all sing because our hearts sing. The heart rises and falls like the sound of music. That is just what a heart does. Perhaps we learned to make music by imitating the sounds around us, but I wonder if we weren't moved to do that because the heart sings, and it longs to hear its own song. Maybe that's why Beethoven could still compose music when his ears could no longer hear it.

Beethoven was in his early twenties when his deafness began. How did he manage to compose such remarkable music as the early stages of tinnitus filled his hearing with a ringing noise or a high-pitched whine, whistle, hiss, or hum? I wonder if it was because that noise couldn't drown out what his heart was singing.

As he grew depressed and the silence overtook the static, he wrote a letter to his brothers, confessing his despair at the unfairness of life and his resistance to living into the ever-deafening silence. It was a letter written but never sent. It was found 25 years later, after his death. Over those two decades, he was able to let the music that was in him make its way into the world in more than 100 compositions that ranged from the stormy music of *The Tempest* to *The Ninth Symphony* with its *Ode to Joy*.[30]

Not only for Beethoven, but also for each of us, the challenge is to let the song our hearts sing make its way into the world, allowing the feelings, insights, intuitions, experiences, and intelligence that sing within us become the song we sing in the world. It might be a song we sing with our hands, with our feet, with our minds, with our skill, with our education, or with our voice. In whatever way it finds expression, it is our hearts' song.

Hearing the song the heart sings takes practice. And translating the song in our heart into the song we live takes practice. Sometimes the heart sings the blues when we are filled with inexplicable or entirely explicable sadness. Sometimes it sings a ballad, trying to make meaning of all the different verses we have written with our lives. Sometimes our heart sings a hymn, singing its praise of life. Sometimes it sings a love song, other times a lament or a requiem. Sometimes it just hums a wordless tune because the soul must sing and has no language for the beauty or heartbreak it is experiencing.

Each river has its own song. It is the nature of water and rocks to sing together. The ocean drums. As the poet of the psalm wrote, "All the trees of the forest sing for joy."[31] We hear their haunting song in the music that comes out of the rub of their entwinement. The leaves sing their new green until the tune changes to the dry rustle of letting go in the fall.

It has often been said that to sing is to pray.[32] The enduring wisdom of so many spiritual traditions teaches us that life asks for our song, for our prayer. Life invites us – through the coming and going of light, through the diminishments, deafness, and competing noises within us and around us – to hear the song within us and make all the music we can for as long as we can.

Of course, it takes practice. And it helps to practice with each other. We come together in spiritual communities as music-making instruments to sing together, pray together, seek wisdom together, and hold stillness together. Together we listen to the song the universe sings, and we find the song that is ours to sing. May we be faithful to that song.

This reflection was offered on May 24, 2015, on the day my friend and predecessor, Rev. Robert Hetherington, a beloved singer among us, became song.

The Practice of Recognition

*The other day when I was making biscuits
folding the dough, pressing the heel of my hand
in the flesh, letting my skin enter that living mass
of flour and milk, baking powder and lard,
enjoying the sensual pleasure of work.
... I felt a shiver of recognition
a stirring of the blood, a blurring of the eyes,
And I was my great great grandmother ...
For that transparent moment I was split
like an atom of pure energy
into more than one woman
in more than one kitchen
alive in more than one history
I was left feeling elated and empty
and put the biscuits in the hot oven ...
We touch the universal and are changed
We touch the particular – bread, bowl or basket
and are transformed.*[33]

~ Mary Woodbury ~

As they came near [Emmaus], he walked ahead as if he were going on. But they urged him strongly, saying, "Stay with us, because it is almost evening and the day is now nearly over." So he went in to stay with them. When he was at the table with them, he took bread, blessed and broke it, and gave it to them. Then their eyes were opened, and they recognized him; and he vanished from their sight. They said to each other, "Were not our hearts burning within us while he was talking to us on the road, while he was opening the scriptures to us?" Luke 24:28-32

There is not one of us who has not walked the road to Emmaus. Emmaus is wherever we go to just get away from it all. Emmaus is whatever we do or wherever we go to escape our greatest hurts and deepest disappointments, even if just for a moment.

In the world of the ancient story, Emmaus is an imaginary village, about seven dusty miles from Jerusalem, a village we've never heard of, a village mentioned nowhere else in the Bible. It is a village that scholars and archeologists have not been able to identify. I recall a lecture in which John Dominic Crossan, a contemporary New Testament scholar, suggested that Emmaus is nowhere because Emmaus is everywhere.

Emmaus is a story that never happened and is always happening,[34] just like the story set on road that goes down from Jerusalem to Jericho – a story of a victim who is helped by an unlikely Samaritan. The famed story of the good Samaritan is a story that never happened and is always happening. These are stories that speak something about the truth of our experience rather than relating an event in history.

In the Emmaus story, two friends are seeking to avoid the pain of seeing the world go about its business as though nothing had happened. They walk in search of the simplicities of village life. They speak of the horrific death they have witnessed and the rumors of their teacher's missing body. Footsteps approach from behind, and a stranger intrudes into their private grief. It takes too much effort to explain their broken hopes. Impatiently, one of them rejects the intruder: "Are you the only one in the country who doesn't know the terrible and tragic things that have happened in Jerusalem this week?"[35]

It is an experience we've all had with a cashier, a driver, or a stranger who has no idea of the meteor that has struck our lives. They inhabit a different world than the one in which our grief has placed us. In this story, the stranger who walks with them becomes a sensitive listener and invites them to share their grief, tell their stories, and speak of the reality they have left the city to escape.

The flood gates of pain open. The beloved is named. The anger toward the enemy who executed their friend is spoken. They give expression to their disappointed hopes for Jesus, his refusal to be the messiah they longed for, and their utter confusion at the irrational news that his body could not be found.

As the stranger places their story amid all that is sacred to them, a compelling pattern emerges. They were close to their destination, but the stranger appears to be going further. They urge him to stay. Around the dinner table, the conversation continues. Following the deepest instinct in grief, they seek to find meaning in the midst of all that has happened. With simple deliberation, the stranger takes bread, blesses, breaks, and shares it. As one ordinary moment follows the next, the deceptive simplicity assumes a shattering significance.

It is next to impossible to share a table and remain anonymous. As we eat together, we become known. The stranger is strangely familiar. And then there is the moment of profound knowing, the inexplicable "aha" – a recognition. When this story was written, some 50 years or more after their teacher had died, the early Jesus community was recognizing that in opening to our common humanity with a stranger, sharing sacred stories, and putting our feet under the same table, the way of Jesus continues. It offers one of our best hopes for healing our hearts and our humanity.

This story reminds us that we are all mystics. We stumble into insights that are quantum transformations, insights that connect us to a deep truth in the universe. We all have these moments described by the poet Mary Woodbury as "a shiver of recognition, a stirring of the blood, a blurring of the eyes."[36] It is not about seeing a ghost or stumbling on a reincarnation of someone we love. It is about recognizing the truth of something that has transformed us.

Some years ago, my friend, Gwen, died in her early thirties. Her husband was left to raise their two young children, both under the age of five. I think Gwen's death was the first experience I had of losing a contemporary. Most deaths I had experienced to that point in my life were from a generation or two ahead of me. A year or two after Gwen died, I was at a cocktail party in a crowded room of law colleagues when I saw the back of someone's head that reminded me of Gwen. In that moment, I was transported in my memory from that room humming with conversation to the pews of Garneau United Church where I often saw the back of Gwen's head on Sunday mornings.

I knew this woman was not Gwen, but I had to follow her around the room in the hope of seeing her face. It was like that moment in the story when the travelers recognized something familiar in the gesture of the stranger blessing, breaking, and sharing bread with them. They wanted to hold onto that shiver of recognition, but it is shattered by the reality that this is the gift of a moment, a moment we can inhabit but can't hold. It doesn't allow us to build a monument or a cairn. It is a moment of insight, recognition, or familiarity. It is a moment of memory or meaning, arriving like a butterfly to comfort and instruct, and then it is gone, leaving us with its yellow residue, the lingering legacy of recognition. It is a moment of awareness, an "aha," a flash of truth about something or someone who has touched us deeply and changed us forever.

While I didn't get to see the face I longed to see in that room, in the gift of that mystical moment, I faced a truth about my vocation. In that transparent moment, I was transported back to the ministry of accompaniment I had shared with Gwen: walking with her through her final illness, providing spiritual care to her family, and celebrating her abbreviated life. This moment shimmered with the memory of the meaning I had found in my earlier years of pastoral ministry, fulfilment that I hadn't found in my subsequent legal career. The memory of Gwen, evoked by this stranger, made me realize that life is too short to spend it wanting to be somewhere else, doing something else. Sometimes these moments of recognition are not about others, they are about recognizing something within ourselves.

A few years after my ordination, I was leading a service in my first parish. We didn't have a lot of musical gifts in that congregation and always welcomed opportunities for special music when a stranger, someone from outside the congregation, came to share those gifts with us. One weekend a young couple in the congregation had a friend visiting who played guitar and sang her own compositions. She offered to share her music with us on Sunday. As she stood before the congregation, strumming her guitar, she stopped and said, "When I heard the news this morning about the U.S. Marines that were killed in Lebanon, I wondered to myself how many of them are on their way to heaven right now, and how many of them are on their way to hell." She was sincere, but everything in me wanted to shout that this was an utterly ridiculous question.

In that moment, I had a great clap of recognition that somewhere along the way I had stopped believing in that kind of a divine judge. I had stopped believing in that kind of retribution in another life. I had come to recognize that we create heaven and hell for each other right here in this life. Those Marines had undoubtedly tasted a little heaven in their lives before they met the hell of war. Somewhere along the road, I had ceased to be motivated in my spirituality by reward and punishment, by some kind of eternal stick and carrot. I had journeyed beyond the exclusive claims of much of the Christian tradition – from asserting a unique Christ presence in Jesus to a recognition of the divine sacredness within each of us.

These moments of recognition are transformative in our lives. They prevent us from taking up residence in Emmaus. They return us to the engagement of our own Jerusalem, inspired by the insight, the truth, and the hope that has found us in some unsuspecting moment.

The heart has a deep capacity for recognition, but it takes practice. We have the capacity to sense the transparent moment that awaits us in our joys and disappointments, in our grief and in our gratitude, in our escape and in our returning home to ourselves. Our healing comes in the ordinary moment when we are "split like an atom of pure energy into more than one woman in more than one kitchen, alive in more than one history ... [when] we touch the universal and are changed."[37] May our hearts be open to all that would transform us. May it be so.

This reflection was offered on June 7, 2015.

The Practice of Unsettling

We are waking up to our history
from a forced slumber
We are breathing it into our lungs
so it will be part of us again
It will make us angry at first
because we will see how much you stole from us
and for how long you watched us suffer
we will see how you see us
and how when we copied your ways
we killed our own ...
And you will cry and cry and cry
because we can never be the same again
But we will cry with you
and we will see ourselves in this huge mess
and we will gently whisper the circle back
and it will be old and it will be new.[38]

~ Rebeka Tabobondung ~

Then someone came to [Jesus] and said, "Teacher, what good deed must I do to have eternal life?" And he said to him, "Why do you ask me about what is good? There is only *one who is good. If you wish to enter into life, keep the commandments." He said to him, "Which ones?" And Jesus said, "You shall not murder; You shall not commit adultery; You shall not steal; You shall not bear false witness; Honour your father and mother; also, You shall love your neighbour as yourself." The young man said to him, "I have kept all these; what do I still lack?" Jesus said to him, "If you wish to be perfect, go, sell your possessions, and give the money to the poor, and you will have treasure in heaven; then come, follow me." When the young man heard this word, he went away grieving, for he had many possessions.* Matthew 19:16-22

I recently participated in the Atlantic Seminar in Theological Education. Along with Diarmuid O'Murchu, an Irish, evolutionary spirituality educator, I was one of the theme speakers, addressing the topic, "Free Range Spirituality: A Spirituality for the 21st Century." Before we began each day's lecture, we were led in ritual by Gkisedtanamoogk, an elder of the Wampanoag people of the Algonquin tribe. It was a wonderful and rich experience, grounded in the symbols and practices that have kept his people connected to the wisdom of spiritual teachers from the animal and natural world.

Midway through the week, a participant made the insightful observation that while Diarmuid and I were offering a European, western cosmology informed by the new universe story, there are also many indigenous understandings of the universe. Our cosmology was just one among many. With Gkisedtanamoogk's willingness to become our teacher, he shared the richness of the spirituality that shaped his understandings and that of his people.

A soft-spoken and wise man, he began his teaching with the creation myth that has been told by his people for many generations. He moved from that understanding to speak of the tragic history between our peoples, the differences in our understandings of our treaties, and the painful road before us to build right relationship. Our bodies shifted in our chairs. We grew uneasy with the hard truth we were hearing. We missed the comfortable place of the mythical stories that we had heard since childhood and were discomforted by the story of our history with one another. Many of us knew ourselves to be unsettled settlers. The seminar ended in a kind of blessed unrest.

This experience made me think about another wisdom teacher who excelled in unsettling the conventional wisdom and the expectations of his nearest and dearest.

> *Little children were being brought to him in order that he might lay his hands on them and pray. The disciples spoke sternly to those who brought them; but Jesus said, "Let the little children come to me, and do not stop them; for it is to such as these that the kingdom of heaven belongs."*[39]

It wasn't Fisher Price or Disney that created the world for children in Jesus' time. What really characterized the world of first century Mediterranean peasants was hunger, poverty, and having too many mouths to feed. The friends of Jesus try to direct him away from spending his time with those who have nothing to bring to the movement he is building. Yet it is to these unnoticed ones that Jesus says the kingdom of heaven belongs.

In the next story Matthew gives us, Jesus turns away a prosperous, prospective follower by seemingly requiring bankruptcy to join his movement. Here's this first century young man who comes along with an inquiring mind and some moral scruples, and he's got money. So why does Jesus go to such lengths to tick him off? It seems like he'd be just the kind of guy the Jesus movement needs. He's likely got connections, he's got resources, he's got some good questions, and he seems to be a model citizen. But instead of trying to recruit him, Jesus invites him into bankruptcy. All the young man asked was what he needed to do to have a more satisfying and meaningful life. According to the storyteller, Jesus tells him that if you want to get a life, start by taking an inventory of your ethics, and determine what your tradition has taught you about living a good life.

Notice where Jesus starts – smack in the middle of the pack of the top ten commandments. Number six: don't kill anyone; seven: don't be unfaithful to your beloved; eight: don't steal from anyone; nine: don't lie to anyone; and then back to number five: show honour to your parents and respect your elders. Perhaps there was no point in pursing the only other commandment about human-to-human relationship. No need to check on the evil of coveting because this guy likely had way more than his neighbour could ever dream of having.

Jesus' inventory includes most of the commandments that speak to what it takes to live with each other. He doesn't say a word about the first four commandments which have to do with the relationship with Israel's god. But Jesus adds a postscript. He adds a commandment of his very own, a shorthand summary of the five from Moses – "Love your neighbour as yourself."

For some reason, Jesus doesn't need to review the commandments that speak to the nature of relationship with one's creator. This spiritual check up invites the young seeker to direct his attention to his relationship with the other members of his own species, with humanity. Maybe it is because the root of his particular spiritual bankruptcy has to do with the lack of right relationship with his fellow human beings.

If you were a rich man in first century Palestine, you got there by your collaboration with the Roman occupiers against your fellow citizens, or you got there by exploiting the misfortunes of your neighbours. You might have gotten there through a land grab when your neighbour couldn't pay their taxes to the emperor. Generally, you acquired wealth by being a beneficiary of the unjust social policies intended to widen the gap between the rich and poor.

It's not a one size fits all spiritual remedy that Jesus is prescribing here. It isn't that Jesus has some big hate on for the rich or that wealth is intrinsically evil. What is clear is that Jesus saw that what this young man needed to do to get a life was to give his life away – to change his lifestyle so that others could live – to redistribute his wealth and embody a change in social policy. The deficiency in this seeker's life was a direct result of the lack of equity, mutuality, and justice in his social and economic relationships.

Ironically, Jesus' sound byte answer falls on the young seeker like blows from a hammer. He gets five imperatives, all verbs, that sum it all up for him – go, sell, give, come, and follow. He went away empty hearted because he could not release his grip on privilege, couldn't let his heart be broken open, couldn't give up the power he had over others. He wasn't willing to have less so that others could have enough.

I had a young friend with an older sister. The older sister cut a piece of cake rather unevenly. The younger sister began to complain that it wasn't fair, until she realized part way through her complaint that her sister was handing her the bigger piece. As she received the bigger piece, she said, "... but it's fair for me!"

It is unsettling to give up, give back, or give over the wealth that has us thinking, "but it's fair for me." The Jesus our tradition gives us is a teacher of alternative wisdom who questions our ideas of fairness and equity. When Luke introduces Jesus to his readers, he says this is the guy who has come to bring good news for the poor. Luke doesn't mention the unsettling truth that he brings bad news to the rich. He comes to bring release to the captives, which is not good news for the jailors. He comes to recover sight to the blind, not such good news for the Pharisees and scribes who have been their guides. He comes to let the oppressed go free: great news for the oppressed, not so good for the oppressors. He comes to reshape the broken circle, to inspire a social vision of equality, mutuality, and respect. This is unsettling for those of us who will have to give up some assumptions, unearned privileges, and distinct advantages so that the pyramid of privilege can become a circle of equality.

Our first century seeker was looking for serenity, not sacrifice. He wanted to increase his personal satisfaction in life. He wasn't interested in building the kind of peace that comes from right relationship.

We know this guy; we know him well. We meet him on the street, and we meet her in the mirror – for we, too, long for life that is eternal in its significance, life that is deep, rich, and satisfying. At some level, we know his sadness, too. We know it because of our resistance to do what is required. It is hard to relinquish privilege, even when we know that it is rooted in injustice. Even though we want a sustainable planet for our children, it is hard for us to change the way we live. It is tempting to choose the feel good of charity rather than the hard work of justice. We want a different social arrangement without losing our advantage. We want to put peace into each other's hands without having to change the balance of power or redistribute the wealth.

The unsettling truth is that it would be easier to drive a Mercedes through a revolving door or lead a camel through the eye of a needle, because eternal life is essentially a radically different way of living in the here and now. Eternal life isn't about some existential crisis of personal meaning. It is about moving our unsettled hearts to restore the circle.

According to Matthew's Jesus, (with all due respect to the words attributed to St. Francis), it isn't in dying that we're born to eternal life, it is in living in right relationship. We meet the unsettling truth again and again in our lives as I met it in the teachings of Gkisedtanamoogk, an elder of the Wampanoag people of the Algonquin tribe. We find it again in the words of the poet, Rebeka Tabobondung, and in the truth of the ancient story of the rich young seeker. Grief and sacrifice are partners in the sacred journey into right relationship.

This is the time to pause and ask ourselves what must we sacrifice, which is to say what must we make sacred to "gently whisper the circle back?"[40]

This reflection was offered on June 28, 2015, as we celebrated National Aboriginal Day (now known as Indigenous Peoples' Day).

The Practice of Unshielding

We have not come here to take prisoners
But to surrender ever more deeply ...
We have not come into this exquisite world
to hold ourselves hostage from love ...

~ Hafiz ~
(14th century)
"We Have Not Come Here to Take Prisoners"

Naaman, commander of the army of the king of Aram, was a great man ... Now the Arameans on one of their raids had taken a young girl captive from the land of Israel, and she served Naaman's wife. She said to her mistress, "If only my lord were with the prophet who is in Samaria! He would cure him of his leprosy." So Naaman came with his horses and chariots and halted at the entrance of Elisha's house. Elisha sent a messenger to him, saying, "Go, wash in the Jordan seven times ..." He went down and immersed himself seven times in the Jordan, according to the word of the man of God; his flesh was restored like the flesh of a young boy, and he was clean. 2 Kings 5:1-3, 9-10, 14

Recently someone rang the doorbell at our home in South Cooking Lake, which I want to tell you is a rare occasion. It usually means someone is campaigning for our vote or the Jehovah Witnesses are going door-to-door. The fact that Simon, our four-legged security system, was barking non-stop didn't deter the cold caller from making his pitch. All we managed to hear over Simon's alarmed response was that the caller was selling a home security system, something that seemed obviously redundant to me in that moment. Security has been a big deal in our society, especially since 9/11. Making us feel safe when we fly, when we go to work, when we turn on the tap, open our mail, or leave our homes has become a mega industry.

This led me to think about our built-in security systems, like the ones built into our hearts. Somehow our hearts become armed, at least in most of us. We acquire perimeter security that defends us against those who would get too close to us. We have our emotion detector sensors that tighten our throats against tears, increase our heart rate when we're angry, make our breath more shallow when we're afraid, and speed up acid production in our stomachs when we're anxious.

We meet some well guarded hearts in the ancient story of Naaman. He was a high-ranking official in the Syrian army with an impressive resume and a chest covered in medals. He was a national war hero and well-placed politically. Naaman had everything except what most of us want more than anything else. Naaman didn't have his health. He was a leper, suffering an ostracizing and debilitating disease that threatened his life.

By the time we meet him in the storied world, he must have seen every doctor, every researcher, and every potential healer. He must have tried every alternative therapy. He followed every lead, tried every experimental treatment, every pill, every lotion, and every diet. He would do anything to be cured. Miraculously, despite a lifetime of disappointments, his heart hadn't closed to the possibility of healing. His heart was still unshielded to the power of hope.

He was even open to a tip he received at least third hand from his wife. In the last battle with their neighbours, Naaman had taken a young Israelite girl captive and brought her back to Syria to be their maid. And she told Naaman's wife that there was a healer she knew of back home in Israel who could help her husband.

Not knowing how much a cure could cost, Naaman filled his suitcase with cash and packed a stash of hospitality gifts. He even thought to have a referral from his king in hand. Given his proximity to political power in Syria, it's not surprising that he thought Israel's palace was the place to start looking for healing. So he went with a letter from his boss and headed straight to the palace of the foreign king.

The king of Israel thought it was a trap. Assuming that everything was always political, he threw a huge tantrum, believing that Naaman had come to declare war with Israel. The king's heart had a highly calibrated security system, and he was ready to conclude that a request for directions to Israel's prophet, the rumoured healer, was actually a call to war.

What is it about Naaman turning up on his doorstep that trips the king's alarm system? I don't know about you, but I recognize the king's security system. I can relate to his shielded heart. There are those we have set our defences to detect: personalities that get under our skin, those we think are trying to manipulate us, those who've hurt us before.

The king likely built his security system sensor by sensor to protect himself from threats he had met along life's way.

Unfortunately, this time his perimeter security protected him from a transformative human encounter. This could have been an experience that dismantled his stereotype, meeting Naaman as a foreign soldier who wasn't declaring war on his country but had come with his hat in hand to ask for help.

Maybe a genuine human encounter with "the enemy" could have improved the king's foreign policy. But even if it didn't make him a better king, it would have made him a better human. His well-armed heart kept him from relating to the vulnerable, unshielded heart of another.

When Elisha, the prophet/healer, learned that the king had sent the stranger away empty handed and empty hearted, he intervened and invited Naaman to his own home. We need the Elishas in our lives who can break through royal barriers to risk relationship with the "other," even with the stranger and the enemy. We need those who will help us risk taking the outsider at face value, trusting the unknown stranger, or even the beloved from whom we have shielded our heart.

But for Naaman, the prophet's hospitality came to an abrupt end when he got to Elisha's driveway, and the renowned healer didn't even bother to come out and meet him personally. Instead, Elisha sent a messenger to convey the peculiar prescription. Naaman was to take a swim in a muddy river. He was utterly offended. The holy man hadn't bothered to meet him, didn't take time to speak with him directly, didn't hear his story, or even thank him for his gifts. Elisha didn't invite him in for a bit of shelter from the sun after his long journey. From Naaman's perspective, he didn't give him the time of day.

Naaman's anger armed his heart. Who did this shaman think he was dealing with anyway? He hadn't even been given a chance to negotiate. The holy man didn't know how much he could pay and what strings he could pull. Naaman, a five-star general, was being sent away to do something ridiculous and embarrassing. And he received this stupid order from a servant, no less!

His heart had shielded itself against an unexpected and embarrassing route to healing. He was prepared for something dramatic and difficult like a rigorous diet or even something mystical like an incomprehensible incantation. A little hocus pocus he was up for, but not something common like a swim in the Jordan River. Naaman expected something expensive, something sensational. He came prepared to pay whatever it cost, but never in his wildest dreams did he imagine the healer he had travelled so far to see wouldn't even give him an appointment. And he would have Naaman strip down in front of his men and take the world's longest bath in a shallow river that didn't even come up to his knees.

It is difficult not to shield our hearts when our expectations are not met. Naaman's security system almost kept him from getting what he had travelled so far to find. Our perimeter and emotion detection systems often do the same. That which has served us well at some point in our lives has the same power to sabotage us.

Naaman's servants knew him well. They let him stew in his own juices for a bit and then found a way to help him unshield his heart. "If the prophet had given you something difficult to do, you would have done it in a minute, but he suggested something simple and common. Come on, let's all go down to the river."[41]

Somehow (and the story doesn't tell us how), Naaman brought himself to appear foolish at the river. He took all his armour off, emptied his pockets, left his shoes and clothes on the bank, and picked his way over the rocks in his bare feet to the deepest part of the river. He exposed himself to a possibility.

Somehow, he managed to unshield his heart and risk appearing utterly foolish. As the story goes, seven dips later, he could have done an ad for Ivory Soap, his skin was that clean! Life invites us to those places where we are stripped bare and separated from our armour, letting go of where we think security is found to expose ourselves to possibilities we are inclined to reject.

For me, neither Naaman nor Elisha is the real hero of this story. They each struggled to disarm themselves against their respective prejudices. The one who had the most reason to shield her heart was the one whose heart remained open, even to her enemy. The young servant girl, the one the story doesn't bother to name because the storyteller is focused on Naaman – she's the one to watch. She carries the enduring wisdom of this story.

She was taken captive, taken away from her people and her land and made a servant of her enemy. Likely held hostage against her will, she's the one who knew that "we have not come into this exquisite world to hold ourselves hostage from love."[42] She generously revealed what she could have kept to herself – there was a prophet in her home country who could help. Why tell your captor where he can find what he is looking for? Why should she care about the one who has hurt her people and torn her from the ones she loves? How did she manage to keep her heart open, even to her enemy?

Maybe she knows that to live is to be insecure. Insecurity is the nature of life. We have not come here to arm ourselves against disappointment, betrayals, hurts, and fears. Security is an illusion. Ironically, our attempts at shielding our hearts against the realities of life imprison us within our own hearts. To be most alive is to disarm our security systems, unshield our hearts, and allow peace to begin in the only place it can, within our own skin. Until there is peace and wholeness within us, there can be no peace and wholeness between us.

Disarmament isn't just a program for superpowers. It begins within each one of us or it never begins. It starts with a heart that has made a habit of unshielding itself, refusing to be taken prisoner by disappointments, losses, hurts, or fears and resisting being held hostage to hurt. Disarming our hearts takes practice. Each new day is a day to recalibrate our security system and discover how to lower our guard, unshield our hearts, and experience courage and freedom ever more deeply.

This reflection was offered on July 8, 2015.

The Practice of Kinship

The spirit of human solidarity and kinship with all life is strengthened when we live with reverence for the mystery of being, gratitude for the gift of life, and humility regarding the human place in nature.

~ Earth Charter ~

Abel was a keeper of sheep, and Cain a tiller of the ground. In the course of time Cain brought to God an offering of the fruit of the ground, and Abel for his part brought of the firstlings of his flock ... And God had regard for Abel and his offering, but for Cain and his offering he had no regard. So Cain was very angry ... Cain said to his brother Abel, "Let us go out to the field." And when they were in the field, Cain rose up against his brother Abel, and killed him.
Genesis 4:2-5, 8

As murders go, it isn't much of a mystery. Near the beginning of the Judeo-Christian Scriptures, two brothers take a walk. Only one comes back to tell the tale. We are led to believe that the crime was premeditated, and the victim didn't defend himself. The motive we are given is jealousy. The tribal god of the story has exercised deadly favouritism, preferring one brother over another; and in that ancient culture, this god has countered the culture by choosing the younger over the favoured firstborn.

The story mirrors a conflict in the ancient world – the long-standing tension between nomadic herders and settled agricultural communities. One brother, Abel, is a shepherd and the other brother, Cain, is a farmer. The storyteller says Cain's culpability is the result of his god's favouritism in preferring his brother, the herder. This left him enraged as the farmer playing second fiddle. In a clear case of conflict of interest, the story also casts this god as the lead investigator. The investigation takes the form of a single question, "Where is your brother?"

According to the collection of stories we have in Genesis, this is not the first question the storytellers ask. In the previous chapter, the god figure asks Cain's parents, the man and woman in hiding, "Where are you?" The entire collection of stories we have in the Hebrew and Christian Scriptures is shaped around these two questions: "Where are you?" and "Where is your brother?" In the first four chapters of the Bible, we are introduced to the three most significant relationships of our human journey – our relationship with creation, our relationship with our source, and our relationship with each other. These relationships define us and shape our conflicts.

In the world of the story, when Cain is asked about Abel's whereabouts, he responds defensively, "How should I know?" "Do you think I have nothing better to do than look out for that little know-it-all?" Cain does what we all do when we're guilty as hell; he says too much. His defense rests in the single question Cain asks to which the story omits any answer, "Am I my brother's keeper?"

It is a profound question. What is our relationship to one another, to family, to friends, and to strangers? Am I my sister and my brother's keeper? Perhaps it isn't a rhetorical question. What if the best answer is we are *not* our brother or sister's keeper?

To be a keeper is to have someone in our charge. Ancient Israel understood their consolidated sky god and earth god, fertility god and rain god, as the sleepless keeper of the nation and of their lives, a supreme super-being who never went off duty. This understanding was enshrined in one of their favourite songs, "God is your keeper ... your shade at your right hand ... God will keep your going out and your coming in from this time on and forevermore."[43] But the relationship between the keeper and kept is a relationship of dependence, dominance, and submission, a relationship which by definition cannot be mutual. The root of the problem in the relationship with the deity and between these brothers is the lack of mutuality, accountability, and responsibility.

Beyond the tribalism in this story, we are invited to recover an even more ancient memory, a memory which runs deep in everything that is. The energy in which we live, move, and have our being is not a supreme caretaker or sky keeper. The ground of our being and becoming, the source of love and of our loving, is being itself. And being invites relationship, not dependence or blind devotion.

If there is no tribal god who is our keeper, perhaps we are not our sister or brother's keeper either. Perhaps our relationship with each other is as kin not as keeper. I am my brother's sister, and you are your brother's brother. For if we are all kin, there is none among us who is the keeper or the kept. Maybe the relationship that Cain so fatally violated was not the responsibility of being his brother's keeper but the privilege of being his brother's brother.

We speak of kin as those with whom we share a biological or legal relationship. When we speak of our family of origin, would it be more accurate to say that the stars are our family of origin, or the sea? We are descendants of bacteria, relatives of the big-brained bipeds who came out of Africa 60 million years ago. How can our kin be limited to those of our species to whom we are related by the accident of birth?

Jesus of Nazareth radically redefined family.[44] And the community of life in which we find ourselves refines our understanding of family even more. There are those great teachers, like the turtle in Mary Oliver's poem, who would help us learn that we are kin not only with the members of our own species, but we are children of the pond, cousins of the trees, and partners with the insects, birds, and animals.[45] Our survival as a species and the survival of those with whom we share this planetary life may well depend upon seeing ourselves as a member of the community of life, part of the whole, kin to earth and sky, rocks, trees, and seas – part of one earth family.

Around the world, Abel's blood continues to cry out, not for a keeper but for a brother or a sister. The ground is drenched with blood – the blood of so many victims of a violence sanctioned by the readings of sacred texts that go unchallenged. There is a great danger perpetrated by our understandings of primitive and petty tribal gods: violence justified in the name of religious supremacy, violence inspired by understandings of entitlement, violence incited by jealousy and greed, violence inherent in the ideology of believing there is one true faith, violence incited by literalism whether it be Hindu, Muslim, Sikh, Jewish, or Christian.

But violence doesn't have the last word. In a time of brutal and violent occupation, when one percent of the elite owned more than 50 percent of the land, when the state religion and its leaders were among the pawns of an oppressive empire, when most people lived in poverty, a brother was born to us. He was a brother who lived and loved well, leaving us with a legacy of how to be siblings. Jesus of Nazareth showed us humanness at its best, loving beyond the boundaries and borders of his society, embracing outsiders, befriending the disenfranchised, sharing a table with those no self-respecting citizen would bring home to his mother.

He resisted the temptation to meet violence with violence and had the audacity to stretch the orthodoxy of his day beyond simply loving their god to include loving one's neighbour as one's self. He taught us that love isn't love unless it includes loving our enemies, doing good to those who hate us, blessing the ones who would curse us, and praying for the abusers.

To meet violence with violence makes us either victors or victims. It will never make us brothers and sisters. Violence brings either victory or defeat, but not peace. Peace requires right relationship, where the imperialism of keepers over the kept gives way to the justice of living as kin, where enemies are loved into becoming brothers and sisters.

What would it mean to cease living like competing clans and live in a co-operative as kin? Jesus asked: "Who is my mother, my brother, my sister?" It is wisdom that answers the question with a question, "Who *isn't* my mother, my brother, or my sister?"

It is a spiritual practice to cultivate kinship. We can no longer afford to live as Cain's children. If our planet is to survive us, if creation is to continue, we will have to *re-member* our kinship. We may not be our brother's keeper, but if our species is going to survive, it will only do so because we have chosen to become brothers and sisters to one another.

This reflection was offered on July 26, 2015.

The Practice of Curiosity

To be wise is to be eternally curious.

~ Frederick Buechner ~

The Lord God commanded the man, "You may freely eat of every tree of the garden; but of the tree of the knowledge of good and evil you shall not eat, for in the day that you eat of it you shall die." But the serpent said to the women, "You will not die; for God knows that when you eat of it your eyes will be opened, and you will be like God, knowing good and evil." Genesis 2:16-17; 3:4-5

Curiosity has been accused of killing the cat, but it seems more likely that curiosity is what makes their nine, sleep-filled lives worth living. But curiosity is not a trait reserved solely for the feline expression of life. Curiosity is essential to the evolution of our own species. So it's not surprising that when we decided to explore Mars, our nearest planetary neighbour, we launched a roving device named "Curiosity."

Our curiosity has led us to learn everything we know about ourselves and our planetary home. It is curiosity that leads us to look and listen, touch and taste, sense and smell. Curiosity fuels our questions and sparks our learning. It keeps us from being satisfied with what we know and calls us to continue the quest to know more about this life in which we find ourselves. The mythical figure of Eve is the patron saint of curiosity.

The Garden of Eden archetypal story has been a great tool of patriarchy and of fostering a "father knows best" kind of god. But this story we love to hate has lessons too important to surrender to those centuries of misinterpretation made possible in part by Augustine's interpretation.[46] Rather than reading it as a story of the origin of sin, what if we come to this ancient tale as a story about curiosity and where we would be without it? If it weren't for curiosity, we'd be a different species; or maybe we would be extinct by now.

The dominant interpretations of this story have turned it into a tale of an idyllic garden with a villainous snake, a foolish woman, a weak man, and a capricious god. We've read it as a story of crime and punishment, a story of falling from the favour of a punitive, paternal deity. But what if it is better understood as the story of rising into the holiness of being truly human? What if it is a story that honours the wisdom of curiosity that leads to a new kind of consciousness and makes us such a creative creature?

The Eden story can be heard as a once upon a time story where the characters give in to their curiosity, give up their dependence, and become the creative creatures that set out to live truly and humanly in the world ever after. It wasn't about living forever. It wasn't about living happily ever after. It was and is about tasting life so fully that it could be truly lived.

"If you taste the fruit of this tree, this tree that you are so curious about, you will know something more. Your eyes will be opened to a new consciousness. You will have a new awareness. You will know both good and evil."[47] In the story we are given, Eve was drawn to the tree for she longed to be discerning and wise. Adam and Eve ate the fruit of the tree, and their eyes were opened. They the saw themselves as they had never seen themselves before. It wasn't long until their experience of the world expanded from the walled garden to the inexhaustible richness of a world beyond their wildest imaginations, thanks to curiosity and her cousins – courage and creativity.

This isn't the tale of disobedient children and their disappointed and disciplinary parent. It is an important story about the power of curiosity that awakens our creativity to journey into a new kind of consciousness, into self-reflective consciousness, into the kind of consciousness required to make decisions. The fruit grows on the tree of knowledge. Curiosity seeks knowledge. Knowledge expands consciousness and choices. Increased choice leads to more responsibility.

Curiosity birthed a series of choices for Adam and Eve, inviting them to leave the infancy and dependence of the garden to embrace a new humanity in a more complex world. It takes courage to act on our curiosity. It takes courage to accept responsibility for who we are becoming and for what we are learning. It takes courage to be responsible for what the world is becoming. If it wasn't for our curiosity, we'd be a species with a very limited consciousness and a very different destiny.

In the garden story and in our history, we recognize our tendency to resist coming into a new consciousness. We resist letting go of the carefree innocence of having an all-knowing, all-powerful, divine caretaker, and we are reluctant to embrace the responsibilities of the humanity that comes with increasing consciousness. We want to make someone or something else responsible for our world, for our circumstances, for good, and for evil. We want the freedom to be human without the responsibility that comes with being *truly* human. So it isn't so surprising that the story has Adam blame Eve and Eve blame the snake in an effort to evade responsibility for acting on their curiosity.

If we were to celebrate Eve as the heroine of the story rather than the villain, we would see this story as an invitation to mature as a species, evolve spiritually, and become the best that we can be. This authenticity increases our capacity for spirit and opens us to truly be spiritual beings in a human experience. It opens us to life after the garden – living truly by loving deeply, engaging fully, and accepting our ability to respond and be responsible.

In this primal story, we see the earthlings choose to become human. We see these two characters evolve into the fullness of what it means to be the human species. We watch these mythical characters choosing to become conscious, choosing to become responsible for their consciousness, choosing to be like the gods – which is to say, choosing to call forth life. They choose to be part of the creative energies of the universe, to be creative beings, just as the god in the story.

Maybe the serpent was right about human potential, about what is possible in our becoming our truest and best selves. The mystics would tell us that to become more authentically human is to become more divine. Isn't that what we see in the finest wisdom teachers, in those who have lived humanness at its best? We see greater transparency of spirit. We see the radiance of holiness in the highest humanness.

Curiosity is essential to the creativity that continues life's story. If we are to cultivate a spiritual life, we must nurture our curiosity and our creativity. As we open to new understandings that displace our previous knowing, there is no returning to the immaturity and dependence we knew in Eden. We will be forever expelled from the well-known garden into the unknown world.

Curiosity keeps us from taking up permanent residence in any garden and leads us to continue becoming cosmic and creative creatures. But it takes practice to open to our curiosity and cultivate the courage to act on it – to become responsible for what we create and for what we discover. Consider what curiosity requires of us. Where is it inviting us to go, and how can we make it a habit we practice each day?

This reflection was offered on July 12, 2015.

The Practice of Reverence

*I often wonder what it would be like if we dared to love this life ~
the fragile and the vulnerable, the endangered,
daring to be humble before the magnitude of our beginnings,
daring to lean our species into a stubborn and pliant wonder,
until reverence shines in all that we do
~ until we live an economic of reverence,
a theology of reverence, a politics of reverence
~ until it permeates education, development, and health care,
homes and relationships, arts and agriculture
~ a reverence for life, for planetary, social and personal wholeness.
This is our purpose now.
May we do it well, with thoroughness and love.[48]*

~ Carolyn McDade ~

Moses was keeping the flock of his father-in-law Jethro, the priest of Midian; he led his flock beyond the wilderness, and came to Horeb, the mountain of God. There the angel of the Lord appeared to him in a flame of fire out of a bush; he looked, and the bush was blazing, yet it was not consumed ... "Come no closer! Remove the sandals from your feet, for the place on which you are standing is holy ground."
Exodus 3:1-2, 5

There is an etiquette we observe in one another's homes – we remove our shoes at the door. It is a habit, perhaps born of our climate. Taking off our shoes tends to be about keeping carpets clean and floors dry. When we do it in our own home, it's often because we are more comfortable in our sock feet or in our slippers. In much of the world, shoes are a luxury beyond the reach of many. Being shoeless is not about comfort or manners, it is the only way to walk.

It is a very different experience to feel the earth directly under our feet, to feel the hot sand or the cool soil, to feel the smooth dampness or the jagged pebbles with unprotected feet. It not only connects us with Earth, but it also connects us to the vulnerability of most of the world's people who walk without the security of shoes.

In one of the world's major religions, being shoeless is a gesture of reverence. Recently, at the beach in Gull Lake, I watched a group of young Muslims find a patch of ground, lay down prayer mats, remove their shoes, and, bowing to the east, undertake one of the five daily rituals of prayer. I am always struck by the colourful array of empty shoes in the doorway of every mosque where people have come to pray. In a place with few adornments, the empty shoes are a powerful symbol of an essential emptying that opens us to experience reverence.

In the world of the ancient story, we meet the legendary patron saint of barefootedness. Mr. Moses is our barefoot man in Midian. As the tale goes, it started out as just another day in his rags to riches and back to rags life. He was born in the barrio near the brickyards, a forbidden baby born to a Hebrew slave in contravention of the Pharaoh's population control policy for foreign workers. He was nursed by an ingenious mother who found a way to have him fished out of the Nile by the soft-hearted daughter of the Pharaoh. That's how he came to be raised in the palace as the adopted grandson of the Pharaoh, with his own mother serving as his nanny. Doesn't it have all the makings of a best seller in the Oprah Winfrey Book Club?

Like every archetypal journey story, Moses has a major identity meltdown. He comes of age and recognizes that he doesn't belong among the Egyptians because he is a Hebrew. He doesn't fit in with the Hebrew people either because his home hasn't been in the barrio but in the palace. How does he continue to enjoy the comforts of the Egyptian palace, while it oppresses the very people from which he comes?

One morning, Moses dons his lone ranger outfit, steps out of the palace, and takes it upon himself to sort things out between an abusive Egyptian manager and the Hebrew workers who are being mistreated. Believing there are no witnesses, he kills the manager. It doesn't take long for word to get back to the palace, and Moses has no place to call home except at the top of the most wanted list.

That's how he came to be in Midian, or perhaps more accurately, in the middle of nowhere. He does what all the guys in Genesis did when they found themselves in the middle of nowhere; they get themselves to a well, and they end up with a wife. Evidently, the well is where you met people in the ancient near east. Long before you met your mate at the community dance, hockey rink, local bar, or internet site, you met each other at the well. Women had to come there everyday to draw water. In return for fighting off some nasty shepherds who had been harassing the women at the well in Midian, Moses gets a wife and a job. That's how he comes to be working for his father-in-law, Jethro.

It is just another ordinary day in the life of a fugitive shepherd when we meet Moses barefoot. He is keeping an eye out for the safety of his sheep and his own skin, protecting his flock and his freedom. He is moving the sheep to the backside of the mountain in the hopes of finding better grazing grounds. He isn't out under the hot desert sun to take a stroll. He is on task with a purpose and a distinct destination in mind. On this ordinary day, he comes unsuspectingly to one of those times and places where something stops us in our tracks. Something causes us to pause, look, and listen, to see the miracle we are living, to bow before the mystery of being.

Out of the corner of his eye, Moses sees something unusual – what appears to be a bush on fire. There are flames, but the bush seems to be untouched. How many times had he walked that path? How many times had he gone past that very bush and never taken any particular notice of it? But on this day, he is sidetracked by something sacred. He sees his surroundings in a new way, and he hears his name in a new way. There is mystery in this most ordinary and mundane moment. He takes off his shoes to respond with reverence and to approach with undivided attention. Somehow, what is here to see requires bare feet!

Shoes often get in the way of knowing the holiness of a moment, of a place, of our humanness, of Earth. Metaphorically, shoes are so much more than what we strap on our feet to protect our soles from the surface of Earth. Shoes are anything we use to protect or distance ourselves from knowing the sacredness of each breath, of each moment, of life itself.

Language is one pair of shoes we wear so that we can build in distance between ourselves and Earth. We speak of Earth as real estate, land as inventory or property. We think of Earth as a special planet in space, the goldilocks of our galaxy with just the right conditions for life, something separate from us. We speak of the earth as an object rather than *Earth* as a subject with which we have an intimate relationship.

Like Moses, we sometimes suffer from amnesia as to who we are and why we are here. We easily forget the evolutionary miracle of life and the wisdom of our ancestors who knew land and water, air and fire as sacred. Our designer shoes cushion our souls from having direct contact with the ground, and we begin to think of Earth as the storehouse of endless resources for us to mine, mint, manufacture, and engineer. Some of us have come to mistake cement for soil and think bread comes from stores.

Our journey as spiritual beings in a human experience calls us to feel the sharp stones beneath our feet and the cool sand between our toes. To really experience the sacredness of our human journey is to expose ourselves to the wisdom that Earth would teach us. We need to find our place in the intricate web of relationships that allows life to flourish and learn to live with respect for the unity and diversity upon which life depends. We need to find a way to embrace the endless transformations necessary for life to continue and to evolve. We are of one substance with Earth, and whatever happens to Earth happens to us.

Being barefoot helped Moses recognize that he couldn't escape what it means to be human. It helped him to hear that, although he might outrun the palace posse, he couldn't run away from the sacredness of life and the miracle of having been given this wild and precious existence.

Being barefoot does help us be present to where we are standing, to be intentional about where we place our feet, and to walk more carefully. Reverence requires the removal of the shoes of hurry and worry, of preoccupation and inattention, of subservience to efficiency and achievement. By allowing ourselves to be present to what is and to where we are, we see the beauty and holiness of what has become so mundane and ordinary that we normally take it for granted.

In our very urban lives, it takes deep intention to remove our socks, shoes, and boots so we can stop, look, and listen. It takes practice to tune our ears, train our eyes, and make reverence a habit of the heart. It all starts with taking off our shoes and exposing our souls to the deep wisdom that is found in the storm and stillness, desert and mountain, in the lake and forest, on the sidewalk and in the backyard.

I wonder which pair of shoes we need to remove to walk barefoot and deepen our reverence for life "until reverence shines in all that we do."[49]

This reflection was offered on August 2, 2015.

The Practice of Belonging

To be human is to belong. Belonging is a circle that embraces everything; if we reject it, we damage our nature. The word "belonging" holds together the two fundamental aspects of life: Being and Longing, the longing of our Being and the being of our Longing.

~ John O'Donohue ~
Eternal Echoes

[Jesus] entered Jericho and was passing through it. A man was there named Zacchaeus; he was a chief tax collector and was rich. He was trying to see who Jesus was, but on account of the crowd he could not, because he was short in stature. So he ran ahead and climbed a sycamore tree to see him, because he was going to pass that way. When Jesus came to the place, he looked up and said to him, "Zacchaeus, hurry and come down; for I must stay at your house today."
Luke 19:1-5

Every September evokes for me the memory of stepping onto the campus at Dalhousie University decades ago, standing in the doorway of the administration building, and feeling utterly overwhelmed. I didn't know which line to stand in, what questions to ask, or how to register for a class, let alone find the classroom. It felt remarkably like 12 years earlier, on the very first day of school, except then I could count on my mother to negotiate the new and unknown for me.

We all have those experiences where we feel like we are the only one who doesn't know what to do or where to go. It's like somehow everyone else knows something we don't know. We feel like we just don't belong, that we are the only one who doesn't fit. Whether it is school, a new job, an interview, an appointment, a meeting, a party, or walking into a spiritual community for the first time, I suspect we have all known the deep loneliness and uncertainty that comes with navigating the new and unfamiliar.

In a much larger way, we are confronted by the plight of millions of the world's people who are searching for refuge and safety, seeking a place to belong, seeking sanctuary from hunger, drought, war, violence, poverty, disease, intolerance, cruelty, or prejudice. In this particular moment, the migration of so many from Syria, Libya, Iraq, Nigeria, South Sudan, and Myanmar has sharpened our awareness of the realities of the world's people who, for any number of reasons, can no longer be at home in their own homeland. Desperation and courage drive the search for food, shelter, and a safe place to belong. For those of us who are a few generations removed from our migrant past, we can only begin to imagine the loneliness and fear that accompany the deep hope of finding a welcome that will enable today's migrants to begin a new and more secure life.

Into our contemporary personal, social, and global quest for belonging comes the wisdom of an ancient story. The movie version of this first century tale that only Luke's gospel gives us would have to cast Danny DeVito in the lead as Zacchaeus. I can't quite picture who would play Mrs. Zacchaeus, but somehow my sympathies are with her. Imagine the look on her face when her husband arrived home, unannounced, with Jesus and a dozen or so of his closest friends for dinner. What was an honour for her husband created an enormous obligation for her. It wasn't likely they entertained very often. Everyone in Jericho knew her husband, not because he was popular, but because he was notorious.

Zacchaeus was a highly successful bureaucrat in the corrupt system that Rome used to occupy Palestine. To become wealthy as a tax collector meant you had to be extremely successful at charging your fellow citizens not only the tax the emperor wanted, and the payoff required by your superior, but a further amount to line your own pocket. Honesty and integrity were not among the skills any head-hunter was looking for in recruiting tax collectors. Zacchaeus must have been even better at his job than most because he rose to the rank of chief tax collector. He managed to be a poorly paid civil servant who became very well-to-do. He appeared to have everything, but he was looking for something. He was disgustingly rich and desperately alone.

He must have heard things about this Galilean peasant from Nazareth who was drawing crowds around the country. Maybe Matthew, the tax collector who had become one of the itinerants travelling with Jesus, had been his employee. Everyone was still talking about the day Matthew left the tax office and never came back. He abandoned the emperor's payroll and left a secure job to hang out with this prophet and his friends from the fishing industry. For whatever reason, Zacchaeus needed to satisfy his curiosity. Maybe if he saw with his own eyes, he could understand why a guy like Matthew would walk away from a job, where he could make a lucrative living, to be in the company of some poor peasant preacher.

The story has Zacchaeus running ahead to find a place where he could see. He was ever the schemer, looking for a way *to see* without *being seen*. At a height of five feet with his sandals on, that's a tall order. But the crook he was hadn't entirely extinguished the boy in him, and he found a way to be both behind and above the crowd. He shimmied up a sycamore tree to see what he could see. I don't know about you, but I can't remember the last time I saw a boss climb a telephone pole for a front seat. And then, as the story goes, for the first time in longer than he could remember, someone *looked up at him*, someone *looked up to him*, someone called him by the name his parents had given him. Someone spoke directly to Zacchaeus and said his company was needed.

I can only imagine what the crowd was anticipating. I can see them rubbing their hands together, expecting Jesus to rant about the corrupt conspiracy and the evils of collaboration with the Roman occupation that Zacchaeus was helping to perpetuate. They must have been waiting for the outrage Jesus was quick to express about the corruption that was robbing people of their land and stealing their bread and their hope. They had to have been hoping for a display of indignation like they would witness as Jesus railed against the temple authorities who were also ripping people off. Wouldn't they be expecting Zacchaeus to be humiliated, hoping Jesus would knock this bloody crook down a few pegs? Even the poorest of the poor might have paid dearly to see Zacchaeus get what they thought he had coming to him.

Instead of calling him names, Jesus spoke his birth name and invited himself to his home. Can he really be saying what we hear him saying? "I *must* stay at your house today." I need to spend time with you. I need to talk to you. I need to know you, put my feet under your table, and sleep under your roof. I need your hospitality. I need to go home with you. Of all the places Jesus could stay in Jericho, of all the good people he could hang out with, why in the world does this story send him home with a crook?

They hadn't even made it across the threshold of his home when Zacchaeus announced that he had too much stuff, and he was going to give half of it away. As for the stuff he had come by dishonestly, the stuff he had acquired by exploiting others, the stuff he had gotten by using his power to intimidate and extort, he would make restitution to those he had hurt. Attempting to make amends, he would redistribute 50 percent of what he had, and then, in addition, he would repay what he took on a ratio of four to one. He wasn't shamed or blamed into doing any of this. It was his response to someone who treated him with dignity and acceptance, who sought relationship with him.

I suspect it wasn't only Zacchaeus who was changed by this genuine human encounter. After all, the story says it was Jesus who expressed his need of Zacchaeus, not the other way around. Why did Jesus need to be with this guy? Why did he need to receive hospitality from one who embodied the ethic and evils of the very system Jesus sought to dismantle? Could it be the same as our need to have conversations and build relationships with those who are the face of the structures we resist, the values we reject, or the systems we seek to change? Could it be the same need we have to be in the company of those we fear, those we label, those whose actions seem inexplicable to us?

There is something about someone calling you by the name your mother or father gave you, about having your name spoken with kindness rather than with judgement and disdain. There is something about being noticed and being treated with dignity and respect, whether we deserve it or not. There is something about being welcomed, about being invited into relationship, about someone wanting to be in our company, even needing to be in our company.

This had to have been a life-changing encounter for both of them. Jesus was received as an honoured guest in a home most first century Jews would not have entered. How could he not be changed by that experience? And it was a life-changing meal with a stranger that made a philanthropist of a thief. In this simple exchange of a common humanity, Zacchaeus was named again as a beloved child of Abraham and Sarah, as one who belonged to the community of ancient Israel, as one invited to live a life based on justice and compassion. In this space where each invited the other to belong to the conversation, to belong at the table, wholeness came not only to Zacchaeus but to his household.

It is easy for hearts to become small and narrow, for opinions and ideas to harden. Obsessions with security and borders can make us quick to label one another and fear one another. It keeps us isolated, afraid of having the conversations where we would discover our common humanity, our common aspirations and fears.

We stand in a time which invites us to know our need of one another, to know our need of the one who seeks refuge in the place we call home, to know our need to belong. And we will never belong until we all belong. There is great wisdom in Jesus' admission that he needed to go home with Zacchaeus. Our indigenous brothers and sisters teach us that we belong to Earth and to each other. Our African brothers and sisters' teaching of

Ubuntu reminds us that "I am because you are." So how can I be if you are not?

This is a time to pause and consider how we might resist the fear and ignorance that keep us from expressing our need of one another. What does our common need to belong require of us?

> *This reflection was offered on September 13, 2015,*
> *as the Syrian refugee crisis was painfully emerging.*
> *It was also the Sunday that our spiritual community*
> *welcomed one another back from summer.*

The Practice of Turning

*The Great Turning is a name for the essential
adventure of our time:
the shift from the Industrial Growth Society
to a life-sustaining civilization.*[50]

~ Joanna Macy ~

*For everything there is a season,
and a time for every matter under heaven:
a time to be born, and a time to die;
a time to plant, and a time to harvest;
a time to break down, and a time to build up;
a time to embrace, and a time to refrain from embracing;
a time to keep silence, and a time to speak.*
Ecclesiastes 3:1-7 (selected phrases)

One of the gifts of summer Dawn and I often get to experience is the opportunity to hike in the Sierra Nevada Mountains or the Canadian Rockies. In the summer of 2015, we got to do both. One of our longer hikes in the Sierras was the nine miles from our campground at 8,600 feet into a back country high camp where we would spend the night at just over 10,000 feet in the shadow of Vogelsang peak.

About two miles into that hike, we began to climb a series of steep switchbacks through the forest. Amid those seemingly endless turns, I wondered (as I always do at some point in every hike) why we were doing this. Turn after turn didn't seem to be taking me anywhere I hadn't already been. After a mile and a half of feeling like I was forever circling back on myself, we were rewarded with a glimpse of why we do this. As we climbed out of the forest, we saw what we could never have seen without making those innumerable turns through the woods. A breathtaking panorama opened to us below.

One of last hikes we did, near the homeward end of our 7,000 km drive, was Parker Ridge, a favourite hike for many of us who live in such close proximity to the Canadian Rockies. It is just off the Banff-Jasper Parkway, a little south of the icefields. It is a short hike that rises from the road, through a series of generous and gradual switchbacks, to a ridge that overlooks the Saskatchewan glacier. Climbing those switchbacks begins to feel like walking a vertical labyrinth. There is a sense of backtracking on oneself or walking away from the summit you were climbing toward just a moment ago. It is turning away from your goal, much like turning away from the centre, as one does so many times in following the path of a labyrinth.

There is a deception in switchbacks that lets you believe that the last turn you can see ahead and above you is the summit. Unlike the switchbacks in the Sierra Nevada Forest, the climb of countless turns up Parker Ridge is on an open slope, and each turn gives you a view with a new perspective. You can't help but know you are moving higher. Even when the path begins to level out, it keeps pulling you forward because there is more and more to see as the vista opens wider and wider. More ranges of mountains come into view. The Saskatchewan Glacier, from which our drinking water in Edmonton comes, can only be seen if we keep trusting the path.

Mountains are great spiritual teachers. Dawn's dad, who was a great mountain man, and his twin sister exchanged a cartoon years ago that became a kind of refrain for them and for us. It shows a couple of hikers, sitting at the summit and looking at the view below. One says to the other, "If it's so beautiful down there, what are we doing up here?"

We make our way through the twists and turns, over the rocks and through the trees, in order to see what we would never otherwise see. The mountain is a great metaphor for life. These ranges we know best in this part of the world were created by catastrophic collisions, rising out of ancient seas only to be sculpted by the scraping of the glaciers as they moved down the slopes. These mountains invite us into a wisdom at the heart of life.

It is the wisdom we also hear in the teachings of the ancient Semitic sage who wrote, "For everything there is a season, and a time for every matter under heaven." It is tempting to become cynical and sarcastic. Life seems to be just one damn thing after another. Everything spins senselessly. It's a merry-go-round, a ferris wheel, a roller coaster, an endlessly turning wheel. After my summer on the switchbacks, I'm inclined to hear the wisdom of Ecclesiastes as the ebb and flow of a single tide. Life is a series of turnings that draw us on into ever new ways of seeing.

Our planetary home turns around the sun. We turn through the seasons. We turn through laughter and tears, building and dismantling, letting go and holding on, searching and finding, mourning and dancing, releasing and embracing. We turn through emptying and filling, planting and harvesting, giving and taking, fighting and making up, beginning and ending and beginning again. Life is full of seemingly opposing experiences that we discover to be turns on the same path, steps in the same dance, chords in the same song, pages we turn in the same book. Like pages we must keep turning to discover how the plot unfolds, life tugs us into turns we must keep making in order to see what we can't yet see.

This is not to say there isn't beauty where we are. There is holy ground right under our feet, and there is still more beauty around the next turn, more wisdom to unfold, more possibilities to open before us. Sometimes the curves in our lives are gentle, and sometimes the turns are abrupt. Sometimes they present choices, an intersection that forces us to decide which way we will turn. But often the path of life turns, taking us where we didn't choose to go.

The twists and turns are always a journey into seeing. It doesn't require 20/20 vision or depend on good eyesight; it depends on our openness to the path with all its twists and turns. It depends on our willingness to gain perspective. Some see with their eyes. Some see with their ears, skin, or noses. Ultimately, whichever sense we rely on, what matters most is whether we see with our *hearts*. Insight depends on opening our hearts just as eyesight depends on opening our eyes.

There is much to narrow our vision, limit our perspective, blind us to possibilities, trap us in our own tunnel vision, or trick us into believing that what we see is all there is to see. There is much to keep us myopic. The temptation is in seeing the sacred only within the narrow confinement of a tradition and in seeing the twists and turns of life merely as fate.

In order to see deeply, we must open deeply. We must give ourselves to the turns in the path beneath our feet. I don't know if there is any better reason to be part of a spiritual community than this. Somehow, our chances of seeing more clearly, more deeply, and more widely are better together. We join a spiritual circle to cultivate the courage to live with eyes open and hearts broken open, never to close again.

Trusting the twists and turns of life takes practice. It is a habit of the heart. Life being life, there is usually some mountain just ahead, inviting us to see with a new perspective. This is a time to pause and consider where we are on our journey into seeing the possibilities grow larger and the problems smaller, sensing the sacred in our turnings.

This reflection was offered on September 20, 2015.

The Practice of Enchantment

And, if you have not been enchanted by this adventure –
your life –
what would do for you?

~ Mary Oliver ~
"To Begin With, the Sweet Grass"

Vanity of vanities, says the Teacher,
vanity of vanities! All is vanity.
What do people gain from all the toil
at which they toil under the sun?
All streams run to the sea,
but the sea is not full ...
All things are wearisome;
more than one can express;
the eye is not satisfied with seeing,
or the ear filled with hearing.
What has been is what will be,
and what has been done is what will be done;
there is nothing new under the sun.

Ecclesiastes 1:2-3, 7-9

And the Lord God planted a garden in Eden, in the east; and there he put the [human] whom he had formed. Out of the ground the Lord God made to grow every tree that is pleasant to the sight and good for food, the tree of life also in the midst of the garden, and the tree of the knowledge of good and evil. Genesis 2:8-9

Everything is empty of meaning and life is without purpose. That's essentially the verdict on the human experience for the writer of Ecclesiastes. For whatever reason, he has come to a time and place in his life where he is unable to find any meaning in work or pleasure, unable to see any purpose in the rhythm of days and nights, seasons and generations. The wonder that rivers and streams run to the sea, but the sea is never full, is lost on him. For this ancient writer, everything is going somewhere that all leads nowhere.

There is something important about these haunting words of hollowness finding their way into the collection of sacred texts for Jews and Christians. If the test for constituting scripture is whether words inspire, the book of Ecclesiastes would surely fail. But if the test is whether they speak the truth of life's experience, clearly, these words have a place in the collection of writings from which our traditions seek wisdom. While these words may fail to inspire, they describe a fear most of us experience at times in our lives. We grow weary of injustice. The inhumanity we inflict on one another and the pain we bring upon Earth and its creatures cause us to despair. We become immune to wonder, and we struggle to make peace with the fact that life and death have some very necessary arrangement between them. We are grieved by loss and change.

When we read the words of this ancient text, we hear the voice of one who may be in the midst of loss. He may need the grace of time and support to bring a measure of healing and hope to his heartbreak. Or perhaps he is struggling with an inner darkness and needs support and good medical care to help lift the shades that blanket him in the isolation of depression. Perhaps he is spiritually bereft, and he needs some time in the forest to become re-enchanted. When these are our words, when this is our verdict on life, it might be time to place ourselves in the presence of the great spiritual teachers with earth in their roots and the sky in their reach. It might be a time when we need the wisdom of the trees.

Recently, Dawn and I had the opportunity to spend time in old growth forest. We were in the California Redwoods, exploring what has been so aptly named *Avenue of the Giants*. To walk amongst these ancient trees is to step into one of our oldest and most magnificent cathedrals. We noticed how most people began to speak in hushed tones, whispering almost, as we do in the great cathedrals and temples of the world.

You can't even begin to capture the wonder on camera. There is something about being in the presence of these great spiritual beings that have stood in their place for so long (some for more than 2,200 years), reaching up to 350 feet in height as they stretch toward the light. They are resilient survivors with few enemies. Even fire is seldom fatal for a redwood. They are possessed of amazingly shallow roots, but growing laterally a hundred feet or more, they intertwine and graft onto one another, helping to hold each other up. Even the death of a tree is the birth of a log that becomes a nursery for as many as 4,000 species, a diversity of species essential to the health of old growth forest.

Standing there in deep stillness, straining to see where the crown of the tree finds light, it seems obvious why the forest is invariably viewed as an enchanted place. There is mystery where so much life emerges from silence, where the health of each being affects the whole, where we are taken into the quiet and embraced by all that dwarfs us. Reverence sweeps us off our feet. We lay down, look up, and are speechless, our senses on high alert to the sounds whose source our eyes can seldom find.

In the world of folktales, the forest is home to the magical and the mysterious, to the experiences of becoming lost and found. Those who are lost are often found by the quirkiest of characters, encounter both good and evil, and are rescued to live happily ever after. Our hero or heroine sets off into the woods on a journey that will be filled with dangers, fraught with obstacles, and from which they will emerge with new wisdom and courage. The forest is a spirit-filled place where we are changed, a place we return from re-enchanted.

There was a time when the forest was home to many of our forbearers. It was a time when more of humanity lived in an intimate relationship with trees. Now we have to make a conscious decision to go to the woods or introduce something of the forest into our urban lives. We plant our children's first grade trees in our yards. We preserve parkland in our cities. We seek to be in relationship with these trees that have so much to teach us.

The Celts, who, like so many indigenous people, lived in a deep relationship with the natural world, found a threefold wisdom in the trees. The leaf teaches the wisdom of change: life is about releasing and letting go. Branches share the wisdom of growth: life is about ever reaching, always growing toward light. Roots know the wisdom of endurance.[51] To survive and thrive is to go ever deeper.

Perhaps those who gave us some of our ancient creation myths intuited a similar wisdom. In the older creation story, the one that actually comes second in the Genesis collection,[52] trees are primal. They are central in the first habitat in which the human ones find themselves. And in this story, the human and the tree are formed from the same substance, from the soil. The trees were inspiring, enchanting, nourishing, and entrusted with the task of instructing the human what was good and what wasn't. After the element of water, the trees are the first living thing for the human to be in relationship with, and according to this myth, it was from the trees that humanity would learn the particular wisdom of discerning good and evil. From a particular tree, knowledge would come. And in the midst of the garden stood the tree of life.

In the paradoxical season of autumn, the trees speak their wisdom with such beauty and brilliance. Everywhere we look we see the leaf wisdom of change. We witness the green giving way to yellow and red, gold and orange, before the great work of letting go to become the humus from which new life will emerge in the spring. In their branches, we witness the growth of this season. We see how trunks and branches weave their way around obstacles to reach for the energy of light. And we see the tree's endurance through wind and draught, as roots reach deeper having no choice but to deepen. When the time comes for the tree to fall in its place, it will be part of the continuance of life as a nurse log for the next generation.

It is easy to become disenchanted. There are many losses which strip our joy and erode our wonder. But there is a tree somewhere, or a forest nearby, inviting us to be re-enchanted, inviting us to recover the wisdom of change, growth, and endurance. It takes attention and intention to not lose heart.

Enchantment is a habit for the heart to cultivate. Very close by, there is a humble spiritual teacher, waiting to teach our hearts to sing again.

This reflection was offered on September 27, 2015.

The Practice of Celebrating Diversity

Dominator culture has tried to keep us all afraid, to make us choose safety instead of risk, sameness instead of diversity. Moving through that fear, finding out what connects us, reveling in our differences; this is the process that brings us closer, that gives us a world of shared values, of meaningful community.

~ bell hooks ~
Teaching Community

They picked Jonah up and threw him into the sea; and the sea ceased from its raging ... But the Lord provided a large fish to swallow up Jonah; and Jonah was in the belly of the fish three days and three nights. Jonah 1:15-17

Jonah is the Archie Bunker of the Bible, the guy who makes no attempt to disguise his bigotry or hide inside any political correctness. The story that gives us this character is better known by its star wildlife, because if we know this story, we know it as *Jonah and the Whale*. It is a great folktale that tells a remarkably subversive story. It starts out with "and it came to pass," which should be our first clue that we are hearing a literary creation that might just as well have begun with "once upon a time, in a far-off land, there was a certain man named Jonah." Jonah is a comical character created by a clever storyteller who fashions this brilliant short story, challenging the prejudices of his own people without paying for it with his life.

Jonah is a buffoonish, cartoon character who wears his biases so brazenly on his sleeve that the audience is caught off guard, laughing at Jonah before they realize they are the brunt of the joke. As the tall tale goes, he has a vision in which his tribal god sends him on a mission to a town of terrorists; at least that was the reputation of the Ninevites in Jonah's world. Jonah is destined to be the superhero, and the Ninevites are cast in the role of being the evil empire; and we all know how this formulaic story should turn out in the end.

The story begins with Jonah being given a divine commission to go to Nineveh and confront Israel's enemy. Nineveh was the capital of ancient Assyria, which had taken the Israelites captive in the eighth century BCE, centuries before this story was told. The Assyrians were viewed as the enemy to the north, the evil empire characterized by corruption and violence. At least that's what Foxy News and Jonah's religious community had been telling him.

Jonah follows his first instinct and sails for Spain, due west on the Mediterranean, definitely not northeast toward Nineveh. Is he directionally challenged or directionally defiant? The runaway becomes a stowaway, until there is a great storm on the sea. He's below deck sleeping while the sailors are doing everything in their power to survive and save the ship. They are praying to their gods, and they are praying with their hands and feet. They call upon their gods for help, and they work their butts off, throwing the cargo overboard to lighten the load.

The only guy who is neither calling on his god to intervene nor doing anything to lend a hand is seen to be the culprit. The storm has neither moved him to pray nor to lift a finger to help. He'd rather be buried at sea than be alive with any Ninevite, so he invites the sailors to throw him overboard, believing this will appease the god he has so displeased and allow the others to escape being tarred with the same punishment for no good reason. But this rough and tough crew of mariners, this multi-faith mix of humanity, this cast of what Jonah would have thought to be infidels and pagans do everything in their power to avoid throwing him overboard. They work as hard to save this outsider as they do to save their own skin. But in the end, they reluctantly concede they have no alternative but to sacrifice him to the sea.

The sea god is appeased, the sailors and the ship are spared, and Jonah's salvation comes swimming by. It must have been a not so tight-lipped tuna that provided hospitality and transportation for three days and three long nights before letting out the biggest belch in the Bible and upchucking Jonah onto a Mediterranean beach. Now he'd have to walk to Nineveh. The Hebrew audiences who heard this story know their Middle Eastern geography well. They know this is like waking up on a beach near Tofino, British Columbia, when you are headed for Vegreville, Alberta. They would see the humour in this fictitious, fishy story.

Jonah arrives in Nineveh, the place the storyteller exaggerates into a huge city that takes three days to walk across. Jonah is so anxious to get done and get out of there that he starts his little spiel on the outskirts of town. He is still arrogant, moody, and couldn't care less about his audience. All this time he has had to prepare, and he hasn't given a moment's thought to his message or its delivery. He just mutters the world's shortest and most insincere sermon, doesn't make any attempt to identify with his listeners, doesn't tell any stories to engage their interest, and still the response is overwhelming. People couldn't fall to their knees fast enough. Even the cattle repented. And to top it all off, it was the king who led the way, showing great remorse.

At the end of his brief, evangelistic career, Jonah was in a major funk. He preferred the dominant theology – an eye for an eye and a tooth for a tooth – you deserved what you got and got what you deserved. Those were the good old days, when you could count on your god to vindicate the righteous and slay the wicked. Jonah represented the conventional wisdom of the day, hook, line and sinker – namely, the fear-filled rhetoric about foreigners that was sweeping through post-exilic Israel and had led to a period of ethnic cleansing. Jonah embodied these beliefs and prejudices. He bought into the assumption that Israel's god hated the Ninevites as much as he did and surely wouldn't waste good compassion on them.

Those for whom this story was devised assumed that the destruction of their temple and their exile into Babylon had been their god's judgment on them for allowing themselves to be corrupted by alien influences. Some of their ancestors had married foreigners like the Ninevites. Those who returned from their exile came to believe that it was these gentiles who had brought judgment on their nation and compromised the racial purity of the chosen people.

It was a creative storyteller who devised this nautical and comical story of Jonah as a protest to undermine the dominate assumptions of a particular people at a particular point in time.

Imagine hearing this story on the streets of Jerusalem in the fifth century BCE, when Ezra, the star priest of the day, and his compatriots are inspiring a closed border, a Jews-only city. In the midst of a purity campaign to stamp out diversity, interracial marriage, and a mix of religious traditions in what amounted to an ethnic cleansing of the city, one hears this prickly story. We wonder, as the Israelites laughed at this right-wing runaway, stowaway, castaway, did they begin to see that Jonah was a caricature of themselves? Did they get caught in the joke as we did in every episode of the TV program *All in the Family*, recognizing Archie Bunker's prejudice in ourselves?

This comical story challenged their assumptions about the world, about the way things are. It challenged their assumptions about that which they called god and also how they perceived themselves. It confronted their ideas about those who differed from them in race and religion, traditions and practices, in what they wore and how they expressed themselves. It was a subversive little story designed to turn their worldview upside down.

Ironically, this story belongs in the prophetic tradition of the Judeo-Christian heritage, perhaps because it uses comedy as a tool to bring a much-needed wisdom to dangerous and deadly assumptions. It is a story that confronts us with our biases and bigotry. The story was and is unfinished. We don't know what Jonah will do with a god that doesn't support his prejudice. We don't know whether Jonah will remain in exile from the best of his humanity. We don't know what he will do with the god who has just transcended his understanding. Will Jonah open his mind and his heart to embrace the diversity that surrounds him in Nineveh?

This ancient story comes to us as mirror to see the Jonah in ourselves, to see where we exclude, or judge, or fail to embrace another and celebrate uniqueness and difference. Several centuries after this story was first told, a prophet would arise in the village of Nazareth who would challenge the boundaries of race, religion, gender, and class, one who would break all the religious rules and social norms. It is easy to celebrate those who think like we do, live like we do, vote like we do, believe what we believe, reject what we reject. But that's not the invitation of the community of Jesus. The invitation is to be radical in hospitality, celebrative of diversity, to be genuine and generous in practicing acceptance.

We come to this ancient and clever story as to a mirror that invites us to examine the habits of our hearts, to commit to making acceptance a habit, to find a way to bless the strange and wonderful diversity in each patch of earth, each drop of water, each leaf and tree, each you and me.

This reflection was offered on October 4, 2015, as an opportunity to reflect on one of SSUC's core commitments – to celebrate diversity.

The Practice of Inspiring Compassion

Love and compassion are necessities, not luxuries.
Without them humanity cannot survive.

~ Dalai Lama XIV ~
The Art of Happiness

A man was going down from Jerusalem to Jericho, and fell into the hands of robbers, who stripped him, beat him, and went away, leaving him half dead. Now by chance a priest was going down that road; and when he saw him, he passed by on the other side. So likewise a Levite, when he came to the place and saw him, passed by on the other side. But a Samaritan while travelling came near him; and when he saw him, he was moved with pity. He went to him and bandaged his wounds, having poured oil and wine on them. Then he put him on his own animal, brought him to an inn, and took care of him. Luke 10:30-34

This story of the Good Samaritan has been recreated many times as a social experiment. Imagine a social scientist, sitting on a hill overlooking the road that descends steeply from

Jerusalem to Jericho. The hidden camera is running. An actor is lying unconscious in the ditch, looking like he has been badly beaten. Our social scientist is waiting to see what happens.

We've seen these re-enactments countless times. They've been staged on busy downtown streets, on the steps of office buildings, on college campuses, and in a host of different settings to try to understand human behaviour. We have seen the same responses that we hear in this ancient story. There are those who pretend not to see, who do their best to avoid the situation and carry on as though nothing is out of the ordinary. We watch those who can't help but see, and yet, for whatever reason, do nothing and continue on their way. Then we see the one who comes to the aid of the injured person, and we can't help but wonder what accounts for the different responses. What is it that leads us either to avoid, intentionally turn away, or get involved?

Irrespective of our postal code, we all live on the dusty and dangerous road between Jerusalem and Jericho. It is the address of our common humanity. Whatever our particular location, we reside on the road that joins birth to death on this cosmic island which is our home for the journey.

The story of the Good Samaritan is perhaps the quintessential story of the Jesus tradition. This is not to say that he was the first or only person to tell such a story or to teach such an important truth about our human experience. Ironically, this story is only given to us by one of the gospel writers, but it is perhaps the foundational narrative of our tradition and the instrument which teaches a spiritual truth that is the cornerstone of each of the enduring religious traditions of the world.

It is a study in compassion. The first action in the story seems devoid of compassion. Someone was brutally attacked by travelers who took from him whatever they could – even the shirt on his back – then left him exposed to the desert sun and certain death. We would call the attackers thieves, offenders, or criminals. Yet likely they too are victims: penalized by a lack of education, schooled in hatred, imprisoned in mental illness, unable to earn a living wage, or impaired by chemical or physical abuse. They are noticed only when they terrorize the world, expressing their anger by blowing up buildings, hijacking hostages, and victimizing others through varieties of violence. We have rarely focussed on the compassion deficit that underlies these hostile actions.

The story introduces two more characters: the priest and the Levite. They have roles in their society which create certain expectations of them. The first century audience for whom this story was created would have thought of these characters as the good guys. They are esteemed members of the social order. Nevertheless, they are victims of a personal piety where convenience is more important than compassion, safety takes priority over risk, and ritual purity has a higher value than rendering aid.

They are victims of a social order that has lost touch, victims of allegiance to principles not people. They choose ceremonial purity over costly, inconvenient compassion. They are unwilling to risk being disqualified from their temple duties by touching what they presumed was a dead body. They aren't especially bad or heartless people. They are likely contributors to all the major charities but lack a passion for justice.

Maybe they simply took counsel in "stranger danger." Maybe this was a trap to get them to stop, while robbers lay in wait. Perhaps this guy in the ditch just got what he had coming to him for keeping bad company or owing money to the wrong people. It could be a gang war where injuries were merely the inevitable consequences of a high-risk lifestyle. Or maybe they couldn't begin to identify with the one who was injured. They couldn't imagine themselves, their family, or friends ever being the one in the ditch.

And then along comes a Samaritan on Jewish soil, the one who has been rejected and discriminated against in Judea. He does the unexpected. It's the bad guy who does the heroic thing. It is the Palestinian in Israel being the hero of the story. It is the Israeli in Gaza being the hero of the story. It is the gay man rendering aid to the known homophobic. It is the oppressed, urban Black man coming to the aid of the injured, white police officer. Not only does the Samaritan cross the road, but he crosses the boundaries of his society. He doesn't seem to consider that he is rendering aid to his enemy. He delays his journey, risks significant danger, spends two days' wages, and promises to give whatever is needed to render compassion.

This story invites its listeners to be moved beyond their distorting prejudices and embrace a new humanity. It paints a picture of what human life could look like if we could move out of our tribe, recognize we live in the same neighbourhood, and become world citizens. It envisions a humanity where compassion is the supreme value in human behaviour. With this story, Jesus implies that if you want to talk about religion, you've got to talk about values. The ultimate questions in life are not about what we believe, what principles we adhere to, or what creed we claim – but about what we value and thus how we live.

In the gospels, we never hear Jesus ask people what they think, what they believe, what causes they support, what products they boycott, what issues they picket, or which politicians they lobby. Rather he is ever and always inviting his friends and followers into a way of living that is ruled by a radical compassion, enabling us to see ourselves in the shoes of another and treat one another as we would hope to be treated were our circumstances theirs. Together we travel the dangerous road that descends from Jerusalem to Jericho, the road of insecurity and vulnerability that seeks to strip us of our prejudices and fears. Jesus' way is a road that calls us away from personal piety or rugged individualism to establish a new human community – a community of thieves and victims, heretics and orthodox, activists and pacifists.

This is the road where all our neighbours live – friends and enemies alike. It is the road where we discover that there is no such thing as personal salvation. My destiny is entirely bound up with yours. We can no longer save a drowning world by building a boat for ten of our favourite people and pets. We can only save ourselves by saving each other, by loving and being loved by our enemies and friends alike. The road from Jerusalem to Jericho calls us to walk softly and love loudly, to practice a life of compassion.

This reflection was offered on Thanksgiving Sunday, October 11, 2015, as an opportunity to reflect on one of SSUC's core commitments – to inspire compassion.

The Practice of Engaging Life with Spiritual Depth

It is not the length of life, but the depth of life.

~ Ralph Waldo Emerson ~

(1803-1882)

[Jesus] got into one of the boats, the one belonging to Simon, and asked him to put out a little way from the shore. Then he sat down and taught the crowds from the boat. When he had finished speaking, he said to Simon, "Put out into the deep water and let down your nets for a catch." ... They caught so many fish that their nets were beginning to break.

Luke 5:3-6

I was wakened the other night by the sound of a very noisy convention on our shallow lake. The tundra swans had arrived from the artic in great numbers, as they do every autumn in their southbound flight. I imagined them arriving at this place on their long-winged migration with the need for rest, nutrients, and apparently a need to communicate, based on the broadcast

I was hearing. Perhaps it was about the journey thus far, the journey to come, or the sheer delight in slipping out of formation and setting down on the water for awhile.

By morning, many were reassembling in flight and continuing on their way. The conversations on the lake quieted. Those who remained were still and solitary, perhaps still satisfying their hunger. It seemed to me I had been witnessing a spiritual gathering of swans. They were in the great work of their lives. Some young and others old, they were undertaking the long migration that the generations before them had made and those coming after them would make. Each generation, guided by instinct, is always adapting to an ever-changing environment.

On our lake, I witnessed them in one of their places of pause where they found nurture and nutrition; they found communion with one another and with water and sky. They found what they needed to carry on. They were gathering as community, feeding their bodies and their spirits, preparing for what was before them. We congregate in much the same way. We come together as spiritual communities to reflect on the work of our lives, to find comfort in the challenges that we meet in our migrations, courage for our journeys, and the nurture that sustains us in all that life requires of us. In the pause of our congregating, we equip each other to once again engage life with spiritual depth.

Among the swans I witnessed congregating, there were surfers, swimmers, and deep feeders. Those surfing the water were trying to land or get airborne. Others swam with such grace and beauty. Many upturned in the water, their long necks reaching down to the bottom to find anything that would satisfy their hunger. The lake and the time together would provide them with what they needed to take to the skies again.

We are surfers, swimmers, and divers in the ways we engage life. There are times we stay on the surface, measuring our lives by the list of things we've managed to accomplish and making meaning out of our achievements. Sometimes we stay on the surface by choosing not to know, not to get too involved, and by keeping our feelings in check so we don't get pulled in or under by anything. We choose to accept what we see and hear as the sum of what is.

There are times we are swimmers, meeting the demands and responsibilities of life with our best skill and effort, moving with a gentle current. There are also times when we are against the tide, the current is strong, and we are doing our best just to keep our heads above water.

Then there are ways life invites us to be divers, to dig deeper, to refuse to accept the superficial, to look for what is beyond, within, or underneath. We question assumptions and answers that have satisfied in the past. We risk the unknown and let ourselves feel deeply, think deeply. We know that in the depths of the mystery, there is something greater, inviting us to live soulfully, unselfishly.

The ancient story where Jesus used Simon's boat is an invitation to engage life with spiritual depth. It is a call to the soul to put out into the deep. In this story, we get a glimpse of this young, unauthorized rabbi, teaching in his unconventional classroom. When the crowd gets too large, he just helps himself to a boat that isn't being used, so they can see him better and he can make use of the good acoustics of talking on water. When he is finished, he has the audacity to offer these experienced fishermen advice.

Simon is a good sport, and he has nothing better to do, so he heads out to humour the good teacher. To make a fishing story the parable it is, the fishermen who had caught nothing in these waters all night end up with a new problem. Their catch is over the limit, their nets are strained to the breaking point, and their boat is taking on water. They bring their boat to shore, hang their nets to dry, and take up a new life on land.

In the world of the story, something happened to these fishermen out there in the deep place. Something changed their dreams, their hopes, their ambitions. Something came of that chance meeting with a stranger on the shore; a new dimension opened in their lives. From now on, the deep place was no longer in the midst of the sea but in the thick of their relationships with their teacher, each other, and with a new vision for how their world could be.

The deep place was a meeting place that changed their lives, reshaped their priorities, changed their vocation, altered their perceptions, and affected their destiny. In the years that followed, Jesus and his friends became a community that was shaped and reshaped by who they were together, a community that came together and changed one another in ways they would never have imagined.

It is unavoidable – life will call each of us into deep water. It might be a disease that takes us there; it might be an addiction; it might be unspeakable tragedy; it might be breathtaking beauty; it might be utter failure; it might be unimaginable good fortune. Somewhere, sometime, we are each taken to the deep. One of the deep spiritual needs of our time is to be equipped for life in the deep end, for living as part of something more than our short lifetime, living for more than ourselves and our family and friends. By putting out into the deep, we can discover the wisdom we need to live a meaningful life, connected to life's source and to each other. We can discover the sacred energy in which we live, and move, and have our being.

Everywhere we turn, we are invited to connect. Our inboxes are full of invitations to be friends on Facebook, to tweet, chat, or blog. Our phone invites us to text. We live in a world of contacts and networks, while our spirits are starving for communion. We have encounters when what our spirits long for is engagement. We have acquaintances when what our spirits yearn for are companions. We are hungry to meet one another in the same way that water meets land and land meets water. I believe we congregate with each other in spiritual communities because we are hungry for more than contact. We are hungry to be changed by our experience of each other and the sacred in which our lives are immersed.

This first century story and the ritual I witness each year with the swans remind us of our need for those places of deep meeting where we are summoned beyond contact and into communion, and from that communion, called to engage life again with spiritual depth. The deep in us longs to open to the deep need of the world and the deep mystery of life. This is a time to pause and consider where it is that life asks us to immerse ourselves in bringing the fullness of who we are to the world's deepest need.

This reflection was offered on October 25, 2015, as an opportunity to reflect on one of SSUC's core commitments – to engage life with spiritual depth.

The Practice of Authenticity

The moon is faithful to its nature and its power is never diminished.

~ Deng Ming-Dao ~
Everyday Tao

Jesus took with him Peter and James and John, and led them up a high mountain ... And he was transfigured before them, and his clothes became dazzling white ... And there appeared to them Elijah with Moses, who were talking with Jesus. Mark 9:2-4

On September 27, 2015, I marked the 34th anniversary of my ordination. I remember well that cool, September Sunday evening, a month before my 24th birthday. We were gathered into the gentle darkness of an autumn evening in the dark, wooded, stained glassed sanctuary of Melville Presbyterian Church in West Hill, Ontario. Gathered with me were members of my family, some classmates from Toronto School of Theology, three Roman Catholic brothers with whom I'd been sharing a clinical pastoral education experience, colleagues from the East Toronto

Presbytery of the Presbyterian Church in Canada, members of the congregation from my field placement, and the minister of my sponsoring congregation in Charlottetown, Prince Edward Island.

I remember the weight of the hands of all the ordained persons in that assembly being placed on me as I was launched into the vocation that had drawn me from the time I was ten years old. Many of us experience a similar kind of moment, whether it is a convocation speech, the first day on the job, being sworn into the bar or the bench, or being granted a license or ticket to practice our trade or profession.

In the weight of those hands, I felt the weight of expectations. It was the 1980s, and we were still thinking of the church as though it were the 1950s. I was appointed to a new church development on the western city limit of Calgary. The expectation was that I would establish not only a presence but also a new church building in that fast-growing residential area of southwest Calgary. I also felt the weight of expectations that I would find something meaningful to say each week, provide wisdom to help navigate conflicts, and be there to celebrate the joys and sorrows in the lives of my parishioners.

It was a tradition in that ordination ceremony that two charges were given, two sermons in effect. One was directed to the congregation as to how they might support and challenge and share the life of being a community of faith with me. The other was directed to me, as the newest member of my vocational community.

I only remember two things that were said to me on that long ago evening. The colleague who had been my supervisor in my field placement at Melville church told me, "Whatever else you do, be yourself and be biblical." It sounded simple at the time. Little did I know how challenging and costly it would be to engage this advice over the course of the next more than three decades. Little did I know, in that moment, how difficult it would be to *know* oneself and then to *be* oneself. Little did I know, in that moment, that the path to being oneself is neither smooth, nor linear, nor obvious, nor is it instant or easy. For most of us, it probably takes a lifetime to live into the advice buried in those two simple words: be yourself. I have come to think that it is about more than simply being true to one's self. It means being a person of integrity and authenticity, one who is trustworthy, compassionate, and respectful.

Little did I know that living into the second piece of advice I was given (to be biblical) would lead me to completely reinterpret my understanding of the nature and value of sacred texts again and again. Time would reframe my understandings such that I would come to see that sacred texts are everywhere – in film, art, nature, literature, and our lived experience. I would come to an understanding of the Bible as a very human product of two ancient cultures, reflecting their biases and beliefs and containing tribal, primitive understandings of the world. I would come to read these texts critically in the way that one reads any piece of literature. I have come to think that to "be biblical" is to be grounded in wisdom both ancient and new, in wisdom within and without. This has led me to challenge the assumptions of some stories and teachings and to turn the prism of texts, looking for whatever light they might reflect or fail to reflect.

I have long been intrigued by a story, which three first century writers give us, about the transformation of Jesus of Nazareth. It is a mystical story in which Jesus is given an audience with two of the heroes of his tradition, Moses and Elijah. We are left to imagine what advice such visitors from the past might offer in such a moment. The story doesn't give us that detail. It leaves it to our imaginations. The story is set at a crossroad moment for Jesus, as he faces the conflict and crisis of what it means to be faithful to his vision for the world and embody the values he has taught – love of enemy, radical equality, and boundary-crossing inclusiveness.

At this intersection of expectations, with pressures from friends and opponents, the storytellers give him an audience with the representatives of the twin pillars of his tradition. Moses stands in for the law, and Elijah represents the prophets. Jesus had ascended this mountain, seeking solitude and time with his closest companions. With Peter, James, and John, he had gotten away to a high place at a low time in his life. A mountain was typically a place of revelation and discernment in the Hebrew tradition. This is a kind of WWMD-WWED moment – what would Moses do and what would Elijah do if they were in his sandals?

We probably all have heroes we like to conjure up for advice, those whose counsel we would seek if we had some way to access them across the great divide of death, history, or time. Whenever we stand at the crossroads, at the intersections of "walk/don't walk," we long for the wisdom of those whose good counsel we would value the most. It may be a hero of history or a hero of our own hearts. Whichever is the case, we long for their advice. The story gives Jesus a moment of companionship and counsel from which he emerges with the determination to be true to himself and to his sense of identity and purpose.

What I see in this story is a way of modelling what it looks like to be true to oneself and to be faithful to the present. Jesus didn't choose to be a new Moses or second Elijah. He didn't need to compete with John the Baptist or satisfy the expectations of the Zealots, who would have followed him in an armed uprising against the Romans that would have been a suicide mission. He didn't choose to be a contemplative and take his place in the desert with the monastic Essenes. He didn't meet all the hopes and expectations of his closest friends and followers. He didn't choose to be all things to all people, to say "yes" to everything that was asked of him. Grounded in compassion and faithful to a peaceful path toward his vision of justice, he continued to act with integrity and authenticity and let the chips fall where they may.

It takes practice to be yourself. Being authentic is a habit to cultivate. Being grounded in the highest values takes attention and intention. This is a time to pause and consider what it is to be true, what expectations we must set aside, what falsehoods need to be unmasked, what freedom lies in authenticity.

This reflection was offered on
All Saints Sunday, November 1, 2015.

The Practice of Peacemaking

The first peace, which is the most important, is that which comes within the souls of people when they realize their relationship, their oneness with the universe and all its powers, and when they realize that at the center of the universe dwells the great spirit, and that this center is really everywhere, it is within each of us.

~ Black Elk – Oglala Sioux ~
The Sacred Pipe

They set Jesus on [the colt]. As he rode along, people kept spreading their cloaks on the road ... The whole multitude began to praise God joyfully with a loud voice ... Some of the Pharisees in the crowd said to him, "Teacher, order your disciples to stop." He answered, "I tell you, if these were silent, the stones would shout out." As he came near and saw the city, he wept over it, saying, "If you, even you, had only recognized on this day the things that make for peace! But now they are hidden from your eyes." Luke 19:35-42

This story of peaceful protest, the one we usually read on Palm Sunday, translates so easily into our time because we have seen it replayed so many times in different ways. There are many contemporary versions of this ancient story where injustice and the abuse of power are confronted in a simple way: a rally, a march, people coming together in city streets or the town square. The props are always the same: something to wave, something to chant, some symbolic act. And there is almost always the same reaction. There are those who would silence the protest and stop it in its tracks, those who confront it with hostility and sometimes violence.

A few weeks ago in West Jerusalem, Israelis and Palestinians seeking peace in their land took to the streets to protest the policies designed to instill fear, suspicion, and hatred of one another. For me, it felt like a replay of a carefully staged and meticulously timed protest against the policies of an occupying empire. Four gospel writers give us an account of a peaceful march from the outskirts of Jerusalem to the steps of its temple in the heart of the city, over 2,000 years ago. It was a protest that countered the primary ideology of the Roman Empire and perhaps the central doctrine of every empire – you get peace through war.

When Jesus of Nazareth and his friends initiated a nonviolent protest, the religious officials tried to warn him to stop this little demonstration with its donkey and singers before it was too late. So often the keepers of the status quo seek to silence dissent, disperse protestors, exercise force, and use the power of arrest as tools to control those who would question the way things are. When dissent is so highly suppressed, it signals that we live in dangerous times. It tells us there are questions we need to ask ourselves, assumptions we need to confront.

If the singers fell silent and the stones took up the song, could we hear the witness they would bear of all the tragedy they have seen since we humans began to walk on them, throw them, and chisel them? If the stones were to speak, could we even begin to hear the lessons embedded in the layers of uprising and conquest, of family against family, of tribe against tribe, of nation against nation? Would we not just simply weep as the storyteller has Jesus weep? Sometimes tears are the most eloquent form of dissent we have. Sometimes tears are our most fervent prayer for peace.

Occupation does not lead to peace. Making more people poor and rich people richer does not lead to peace. These actions, whether in the first century or the twenty-first century, have all the ingredients necessary to breed generations of violence.

Would that even today we knew the things that make for peace! They are hidden from our eyes. They are not hidden because they are state secrets or among the hidden mysteries of the universe. We hide them when we silence the cries of dissent, when we refuse to listen to the voices that line our streets. So many voices have been silenced. Will we not learn to answer violence with something other than more violence? Fear is best answered with love, hostility with understanding, arrogance with humility.

We will never make peace as long as we make poverty. We will never make peace while we make terror. We will never make peace, if we fail to listen to those for whom the way things are just isn't working. We will never make peace by deploying censorship. We will never make peace by exercising power over another.

The things that make for peace are not hidden in top secret military documents; they are written in every heart. They are the things that all beings long for – food and shelter, love, respect and trust, justice, equality and freedom. They are not hidden or disguised. They are as plain as the nose on any face, the basic dignities of respect and mutual co-existence.

The end of a conflict might give us a treaty. The end of a war might give us an armistice. The end of a battle might give us a cease fire. War can give us these things, but it cannot give us peace.

I have walked the streets of Jerusalem many times. I have witnessed faithful Muslims at prayer five times a day and observant Jews making their way to the western wall at all hours of the day and night to pray. I have observed devout Christians making a pilgrimage through the streets of the old city, stopping to pray at every station of the cross on the Via Dolorosa. But we will not make peace with our prayers either.

It is a great tragedy of misdirected piety that the world's three great Abrahamic religions all pray for a peace that we are not willing to make together. The things that make for peace do not come from any sky god. The things that make for peace are not given to us by winning a war, signing a treaty, or moving any deity to deliver us the peace for which we pray. The things that make for peace are the work of the human heart, will, and mind. They require the hard work of seeing ourselves in one another, seeing the sacred in our enemies, seeing that everything is a part of us, and we are a part of everything. What makes for peace is the most basic of human acts: to treat others as we ourselves wish to be treated. If we were to act out of our truest and best humanity, we would surely know the things that make for peace! They would not be hidden from our eyes.

Peace is not won. Peace is not kept. Peace is made in the hard work of refusing to be enemies by treating one another as we long to be treated. Peacemaking is a habit that begins in the heart. We have achieved the capacity to bomb the world to pieces, but somehow, we have yet to learn that we can never bomb the world into peace.[53]

On this anniversary of the assassination of Yitzhak Rabin, who lived long enough to learn that war wouldn't make peace and occupation wouldn't make peace, but land might make peace, we examine our own hearts for the peace that is hidden from our eyes. As we commemorate Remembrance Day once again, we remember the armistice that ended the first world war of the last century. It is a time to remember the tragedy and failure of war and its unspeakable cost. It is a day to discern just one thing we can do to make peace a habit – in our hearts, in our homes, in our workplaces, in our classrooms, in our churches, and in our neighbourhoods. Surely the stones still cry with their wisdom that we will not know the things that make for peace until we do the things that make for justice. But what does justice require of us?

This reflection was offered on Remembrance Day Sunday, November 8, 2015, when Kathryne Kuhn, a member of SSUC, was presented with the Canadian Peacekeeping Service Medal.

The Practice of Seeking Justice

Justice is the pitch of the roof and the structure of the walls. Mercy is the patter of rain on the roof and the life sheltered by the walls. Justice is the grammar of things. Mercy is the poetry of things.

~ Frederick Buechner ~
Whistling in the Dark

Jephthah made a vow to the Lord, and said, "If you will give the Ammonites into my hand, then whoever comes out of the doors of my house to meet me, when I return victorious ... shall be the Lord's, to be offered up by me as a burnt offering." So Jephthah crossed over to the Ammonites to fight against them; and the Lord gave them into his hand ... Then Jephthah came to his home at Mizpah; and there was his daughter coming to meet him with timbrels and with dancing. She was his only child ... When he saw her, he tore his clothes, and said, "Alas, my daughter! You have brought me very low; you have become the cause of great trouble to me." ... At the end of two months, she returned to her father, who did with her according to the vow he had made ...
Judges 11:30-40

One of the most dangerous weapons we've ever built is fanatical devotion. We'd like to think that the Jephthahs of the world and their victims are relegated to a shameful, patriarchal, and tribal time in our history. But sadly, these deadly expressions of blind devotion and brute force are far from extinct.

On October 11, 2015, in Chadwicks, New York, 19-year-old Lucas Leonard was beaten to death in the sanctuary room of his church by his family and other church leaders. His parents were charged with manslaughter; his sister was also charged in the deadly assault. This violence occurred during a counselling session initiated by their pastor. The beating, they believed, was authorized by their interpretation of the Bible. Lucas' younger brother was seriously injured by the beatings also inflicted on him that night. These teens were beaten with fists and whipped with electrical cords for more than eight hours by members of their church as punishment for the "sin" of wishing to leave The Word of Life Christian Church.[54]

No single religious tradition holds a monopoly on such deadly devotion and misguided piety. Several years ago, the parents in the Shafia family were convicted of murdering their three daughters and the husband's first wife by drowning them in a vehicle submerged in a Kingston canal. The accused justified it as an honour killing. For the victims, it was a brutal and misguided understanding of their religion and culture. It was a death sentence for "the crime" these women were seen to have committed by seeking independence and freedom from domestic abuse and the control of a contorted ideology.[55]

Deadly devotion to an extremist ideology piloted planes into the World Trade Centre and the Pentagon. Deadly devotion has caused parents to refuse lifesaving treatment for their children and led an entire community of women, men, and children to drink lethally laced Kool-Aid. Deadly devotion has persuaded young men and women to strap bombs to their bodies and open fire with automatic weapons in the name of some god whose reward they seek for their service of vengeance.

Jephthah, a character we meet in the book of Judges, is not a relic of the past but a stark warning of dangerous devotion. Although he takes up several chapters in the sacred texts of the Judeo-Christian scriptures, his is not a story we tend to tell in either the synagogue or the church. Children's Bible story books generally jump from the violence and warriorhood of Joshua to the strongman Samson and give Jephthah a miss. It is certainly not a bedtime story any parent is going to want to read to their children.

Jephthah's story is not fraught with moral ambiguity like the stories of some parents who struggle with how to alleviate their children's pain, face their hunger, or determine which child to pick up when you have to flee the horrors being perpetrated on your village. Jephthah's story is a terrible tale of the perils of piety, of reckless religion, of a vow that makes another a victim.

Like the rest of us, Jephthah *has* a story, and he *is* a story. He is the scandalous child, the son of a prostitute. We can imagine the bullying and brutality he faced as a child with something to prove. He was likely the target of the taunts of his legitimate brothers that he was the bastard son of so and so. After their father dies, the legitimate sons cut him out of the estate and turn him out into the street. Jephthah, like so many young men and women seeking to belong, attaches himself to a band of extremists.

Not surprisingly, he finds a bunch of bullies to hang out with and makes a name for himself as a gang leader. He becomes a renowned street fighter, and why not? He has spent his life fighting his reputation, being denied a place in his family, and struggling to survive in a world that rejects him. But when war is on the horizon, he is sought out by the very clan that rejected him.

Now that he can do something for them, he is valuable. When negotiations fail between Israel and the Ammonites, Jephthah tenders his bargaining chip. He will fight for Israel if they agree to make him their commander and chief. How often has this agenda been repeated? A wounded psyche is drawn like a magnet to achieve power and recognition, and when power isn't enough to fill the void within him, he reaches for piety and makes a reckless and irresponsible vow. Power and piety can be a deadly duo.

As the terrible tale goes, his misguided religiosity leads him to makes a grand gesture before his cohorts – when their god gives them victory in the battle, he will celebrate the divine deliverance by sacrificing whoever comes through the door to greet his return home. What seduced him into making such a stupid and unnecessary promise? And what in the world made him keep such a senseless promise? Did he think it was going to make him a hero? Did he think this would secure his place in the community and in history as valiant and virtuous? What *was* he thinking? Was his ego truly more important to him than the life of his only daughter? How could he be so blind to the consequences of his vow? He had to have known that some innocent member of his household, with no stake in his promise, was going to pay the price for his egotistical boast.

With classic cowardice, he blames the victim instead of accusing himself of insanity and losing face. He lashes out at his daughter when she dances across the threshold to welcome him home. Instead of throwing his arms around her and telling her how happy he is to see her, he rages at her and accuses her of shaming him by being in the right place at the wrong time. He doesn't pause for a moment in putting his devotion before his daughter. She doesn't hesitate in putting her devotion to her father before self-preservation. So there we have it – everything that is necessary for devotion to move from dangerous to deadly. This unnamed child becomes a victim of her father's foolish vow.

There are countless victims of blind zeal, mindless piety, or religion that lacks integrity and compassion. There are countless victimizers who were once victims. Many perpetrators of violence are also wounded spirits who have been abused and misused, neglected or mistreated. The *REDress Project*[56] remembers the more than 1,100 missing and murdered indigenous women and girls who have been lured, overpowered, mistreated, and murdered, possibly by men like Jephthah who were victims before they became victimizers.

Recently, we have witnessed horrors in Baghdad, Beirut, Paris, and Kenya, among others, horrific acts sparked by religious fanaticism – the Jephthah story replayed in its twenty-first century version. The world is quick to dismiss the perpetrators of such horror as barbarians, but they are human beings who have a story we need to hear before they become the headline we hate to hear.

In the world of this ancient, tragic tale, before she became the victim of her father's vow, Jephthah's daughter sought and received a reprieve. She was given two months in which to live a lifetime and mourn a senseless and premature death. She did not choose to do this alone, but in community with her companions. They were all as vulnerable as she was to the tribal religion of their fathers and mothers, to being sacrificed by a society adhering to a perverted religion.

From the viewpoint of my safe, white, western, middle class, protected childhood and privileged life, I will never understand why she returned. But I have not walked in her sandals. I don't know what it is to live in an abusive relationship. I'm sure there are many who know exactly why she had no power to do otherwise. Sadly, there are those who deeply understand why she saw no alternative but to submit to her father's fatal ego and distorted devotion to his god.

What I do understand is the power of the tradition that her story inspired among the daughters of Israel. For four days each year, they apparently devoted themselves to preserving her memory.[57] It is like the community we form annually across Canada on December 6th to preserve the memory of the women of the Montreal Massacre, and the community of memory we form in performance art when we participate in the *REDress Project*.

These are ways we, as women and men and children, carry on the tradition of the daughters of Israel in the power of our lament, the power of memory. We share vigils, build memorials, and create art to inspire ourselves to better ways, refusing to repeat the atrocities of the past. We devise practices to prevent devotion being defined by extremists and insanity. It requires vigilance to challenge any religion that requires such deadly devotion. We must resist the scapegoating that chooses to blame the victim for the length of her skirt or the risks of her livelihood. And we must refuse the tendency to see the one who harms merely as victimizer, an incarnation of evil, or something other than human.

A community that seeks to teach and honour a deep respect for life has the power to restore one another to self-respect, reimagining justice not as revenge or punishment but as healing and restoration. There will always be those few whose humanity is so broken that it is beyond healing. But there are many who have been harmed and who have inflicted harm whose deepest healing can happen in the transformative power of empathy, forgiveness, and reconciliation.

Honouring the value of each life is a habit of the heart. Justice-making takes practice. It requires healing. It needs compassion. It insists on accountability. It takes all of us. It begins when we seek to listen and resist revenge. It begins when we refuse to confuse retaliation and punishment with justice. For there can be no justice without a deep and abiding respect for life.

This reflection was offered on November 15, 2015, honouring Restorative Justice Week in Canada.

Epilogue

When I became a member of the Law Society of Alberta, I recognized in that moment that I was beginning to practice law. I was a newly minted lawyer. But the truth of the matter was that whether I had been a lawyer for five minutes or fifty years, I would just be practicing. I would only, ever, and always be a practitioner – one continuously learning, adapting, and applying legal principles, codified and common law to the ever-evolving circumstances and situations in life.

The same is true for the medical profession. Whether you are a generalist or a specialist, physicians practice medicine. If we are honest about it, we could say the same things about most trades and professions. They are, at best, the application of a particular skill in a variety of situations, and whether we're teaching, nursing, plumbing, engaging in engineering or in ministry, we are practitioners. And the work that we do is a practice.

In the world of sports, it is inconceivable that one would ever play without investing hours in practicing. When we see great talent in hockey, we know that the skill is the result of immeasurable hours of practice. When we hear a great orchestra perform or see a play or go to a gallery, we know that our eyes and our ears are reaping the reward of someone's extraordinary investment in their practice.

But I have more recently come to realize that it takes practice to keep human life human. It takes practice to be most deeply, fully human. To be spiritually awake in our human experience requires practice. To be a person of faith or a spiritual seeker is not about making any profession of faith or holding particular beliefs. It is to be committed to the practices that keep our hearts pliable with wonder, tender with compassion, and responsive to the pain and joys of the world.

As I have revisited and revised these reflections to share with you, my hope is that among and beyond these practices you will find some of the habits you need to build the muscle of faithfulness and resilience for living truly and loving deeply – to be a spiritual seeker committed to the practice of honing our highest humanity and our deepest divinity.

Notes

1. The nature of this spiritual community is well expressed in its identity statement. "We are spiritual seekers united in community: celebrating diversity, making a positive difference, inspiring compassion, and engaging life with spiritual depth." See http://www.ssucedmonton.com.

2. *The Trevor Project* (https://www.thetrevorproject.org/) was founded in 1998 by the creators of the Academy Award-winning short film, "Trevor." It is a leading national organization providing crisis intervention and suicide prevention services to lesbian, gay, bisexual, transgender, queer, and questioning (LGBTQ2S+) young people under 25. See the video on vulnerability. AppleEmployees, "It Gets Better: Apple Employees," April 13, 2011, YouTube video, 6:03, https://www.youtube.com/watch?v=iWYqsaJk_U8.

3. The movie *Frozen* is a 2013 American, computer-animated, musical fantasy film produced by Walt Disney Animation Studios and released by Walt Disney Pictures.

4. "We are not human beings having a spiritual experience. We are spiritual beings having a human experience." This expression is commonly attributed to Pierre Teilhard de Chardin, but the attribution has been questioned and cannot be verified. I have restated this idea throughout this collection as "we are spiritual beings in a human experience" to reflect my own understanding of the essence of our humanity.

5   The *Charter for Compassion* can be found at https://charterforcompassion.org. With funding and support from the TED organization, under the leadership of Karen Armstrong, a *Charter for Compassion* was crafted by a group of leading inspirational thinkers from the traditions of Judaism, Christianity, and Islam and based on the fundamental principles of universal justice and respect. In 2009, the Charter was born. It grew from the contributions of more than 150,000 people from 180 countries and was crafted into a succinct, 312-word pledge that allows room for all faiths.

6   On August 28, 2012, in a 62-page verdict, Judge Oded Gershon ruled that Corrie's death was an accident for which she was responsible and absolved the Israeli Defense Force (IDF) of any wrongdoing. In February 2015, the Israeli Supreme Court upheld this finding, dismissing the appeal by the Corrie family. See http://rachelcorriefoundation.org.

7   The Amplified Bible, Aramaic Bible, and Brenton Septuagint Translation use the phrase "hearing heart" or "a heart to hear" rather than the NRSV translation of "understanding mind."

8   *Unfinished Song* is a 2012 award-winning British film (with the original title *Song for Marion*) about a grieving pensioner who finds comfort and healing in the local choir that had been a source of community for his wife prior to her death.

9   A paraphrase emphasizing the form of the text found in Matthew 5:21-48.

10 These are the affirmations and intentions shared in each celebration of baptism at SSUC.

11 These phrases outline the identity statement of SSUC.

12 SSUC has adopted these principles of the *Earth Charter*. See https://earthcharter.org.

13 In 1999, SSUC became the first affirming ministry of the United Church of Canada in Alberta.

14 In 1967, when SSUC was formed, one of the founding commitments was to a be a church without walls. For the next 32 years, the congregation utilized schools and community centres as its gathering place. Just before the turn of the century, SSUC determined that it could best serve the community by building a multipurpose facility that could be a place of hospitality for diverse programs and services for a growing population in south Edmonton. The doors were first opened in March 2000.

15 For more on the work of Angeles Arrien, see https://charterforcompassion.org/the-legacy-of-angeles-arrien.

16 This reflection draws on the work of Marcus J. Borg and John Dominic Crossan, *The Last Week: A Day-by-Day Account of Jesus's Final Week in Jerusalem* (New York: HarperSanFrancisco, 2006), 2-30.

17 Paraphrase of Luke 24:6.

18 Jack Layton, "Jack Layton's Last Letter to Canadians," August 20, 2011 (Toronto: CBC News, August 22, 2011). https://www.cbc.ca/news/politics/jack-layton-s-last-letter-to-canadians-1.991992.

19 This illustration and many like it are widely available on the internet.

20 June Jordan, "Poem for South African Women," *Passion* (Port Townsend, Washington: Copper Canyon Press, 2021, [first published, 1980]). http://www.junejordan.net/poem-for-south-african-women.html. Jordan has been widely credited for coining this phrase. In 2006, Alice Walker picked it up as a title for her book. *Sweet Honey in the Rock* turned it into a song.

Barack Obama evoked both controversy and inspiration when he spoke these words on the campaign trail.

21 Paraphrase of Mark 8:36.

22 Though this attribution to Abraham Joshua Heschel is widely found on the internet, an original source is not cited.

23 For a deeper understanding of the new universe story, see Brian Thomas Swimme and Mary Evelyn Tucker, *Journey of the Universe* (New Haven, Connecticut: Yale University Press, 2011).

24 This phrase is used by many indigenous peoples as an expression of their understanding that everything in the web of creation is interdependent and connected.

25 These miracles of ancestry that I introduce here are developed more fully and poetically by Forrest Church, *Love and Death: My Journey Through the Valley of the Shadow* (Boston: Beacon Press, 2009) 101-105.

26 Dawna Markova, "Wide Open," © Dawna Markova, Ph.D, 2022. Cited with permission of the author.

27 Markova, "Wide Open."

28 Barbara Brown Taylor, *An Altar in the World: A Geography of Faith* (New York: HarperOne, 2009), 123.

29 Mary Oliver, "Invitation," *Red Bird* (Boston: Beacon Press, 2008), 18-19.

30 To read Beethoven's story in much more detail, see Mark Nepo, *Seven Thousand Ways to Listen: Staying Close to What is Sacred* (New York: Free Press, 2012), 142-147.

31 Psalm 96:12.

32 "He who sings prays twice" is commonly attributed to St. Augustine (354-430 CE), but the attribution has been questioned and cannot be verified.

33 Mary Woodbury, "Transfiguration," *Still Life at Seventy* (Edmonton, Alberta: Talkingstick Press, 2013), 120-121. Cited with permission by the literary executor of the author.

34 John Dominic Crossan, *Jesus: A Revolutionary Biography* (New York: HarperSanFrancisco, 1994), 197.

35 Paraphrase of Luke 24:18.

36 Woodbury, "Transfiguration."

37 Woodbury, "Transfiguration."

38 Rebeka Tabobondung, Excerpt from "Reconciliation," *Muskrat Magazine,* Issue 18, New Generation, September 2021. The entire poem is available at http://muskratmagazine.com/reconciliation-feature-poem/. Cited with permission of the author.

39 Matthew 19:13-14.

40 Rebeka Tabobondung, "Reconciliation."

41 Paraphrase of 2 Kings 5:13.

42 Hafiz (also known as Hafez), "We Have Not Come Here to Take Prisoners," *The Gift: Poems by Hafiz, the Great Sufi Master*, translated by Daniel Ladinsky (New York: Penguin Books, 1999).

43 Psalm 121:5, 8.

44 "Who are my mother and my brothers?" And looking at those who sat around him, [Jesus] said, "Here are my mother and my brothers! Whoever does the will of God is my brother and sister and mother." Mark 3:33-35.

45 Mary Oliver, "The Turtle," *Dream Work* (New York: The Atlantic Monthly Press, 1986), 57-58.

46 Christianity had no doctrine of "original sin" prior to the fourth century. St. Augustine of Hippo (354-430 CE) was the first to use this phrase.

47 Paraphrase of Genesis 3:5.

48 Carolyn McDade, *Through the Moons of Autumn: Witness to the Land on which I Live* (Wellfleet, Massachusetts: Carolyn McDade, 1995). Cited with permission of the author.

49 McDade, *Through the Moons of Autumn.*

50 Joanna Macy, https://www.ecoliteracy.org/article/great-turning.

51 Inspired by "Elemental Tree," a greeting card by Jen Delyth, http://www.celticartstudio.com.

52 The older creation story begins at Genesis 2:4b.

53 Michael Franti, "Bomb the world," September 24, 2008, YouTube video, 4:35, https://www.youtube.com/watch?v=VILqFtrzBxA.

54 See https://www.washingtonpost.com/news/acts-of-faith/wp/2015/10/22/it-hurt-everywhere-teen-talks-about-deadly-beating-at-reclusive-n-y-church/.

55 See https://www.macleans.ca/news/canada/inside-the-shafia-killings-that-shocked-a-nation/.

56 The REDress Project began as a public art installation created by Jaime Black in response to the epidemic of missing and murdered Indigenous women (MMIW) in Canada. This project inspires the hanging of empty red dresses in a range of environments across the country. See https://www.jaimeblackartist.com/exhibitions/.

57 Judges 11:39-40.

About the Artist

The book cover design is by Amy Loewan, a visual artist based in Edmonton, Alberta, Canada. She received a Master of Fine Arts degree in Painting from the University of Alberta and is a member of the Royal Canadian Academy of Arts.

Amy is celebrated for her dedication to creating artwork that promotes peace, harmony, and understanding. In designing this book cover, Amy focused on the use of colour and symbol to evoke the contemplative spirit in order to reach the human heart. To learn more about Amy's art and view some of her community projects and large installations, visit:

http://www.amyloewan.com

About the Author

Nancy's early life was shaped by the land where the confluence of Indigenous, Anglophone and Francophone peoples make their homes along the Restigouche River in northern New Brunswick. The spiritual landscape of her childhood and adolescence was the world of evangelicalism. After obtaining a B.Sc. at Dalhousie University and completing her theological studies in southern California, Nancy found a home, for a time, in the reformed tradition, providing leadership to a spiritual community in the foothills of the Canadian Rockies in Calgary, Alberta.

In 1986, she migrated north to Edmonton to study law at the University of Alberta. After completing her law degree and articles with the federal Department of Justice, she worked as a crown prosecutor before opening her own private practice in civil and criminal law. Since 2003, Nancy has been part of the leadership team of Southminister-Steinhauer United Church (SSUC) in Edmonton, Alberta, a progressive community of spiritual seekers.

Nancy received a Doctor of Ministry from Chicago Theological Seminary in 2009. Her thesis focused on "Setting a Spacious Table: A Model for Preaching an Expansive Theology." Having migrated from her evangelical roots and the reformed tradition, Nancy explores an expansive spirituality that honours her beginnings in the Judeo-Christian household but reaches beyond it to the wisdom of other enduring spiritual traditions, the natural world, poetry, the arts, and science. Nancy and her spouse, Dawn, continue their evolutionary journey from dogma and doctrine, beyond the confines of a creed, to a spirituality that celebrates diversity and finds its ground in values that enhance life for Earth, its peoples and creatures.

To order more copies of this book, find books by other
Canadian authors, or make inquiries about publishing your
own book, contact PageMaster at:

PageMaster Publication Services Inc.
11340-120 Street, Edmonton, AB T5G 0W5
books@pagemaster.ca
780-425-9303

catalogue and e-commerce store
PageMasterPublishing.ca/Shop

www.ingramcontent.com/pod-product-compliance
Lightning Source LLC
Chambersburg PA
CBHW070048100426
42734CB00040B/2727